The
Garland Library
of
War and Peace

The
Garland Library
of
War and Peace

Under the General Editorship of
Blanche Wiesen Cook, *John Jay College, C.U.N.Y.*
Sandi E. Cooper, *Richmond College, C.U.N.Y.*
Charles Chatfield, *Wittenberg University*

Fighting for Peace

The Story of the War Resistance Movement

by

William Joseph Chamberlain

with a foreword by

Harold J. Morland

with a new introduction
for the Garland Edition by

Larry Gara

Garland Publishing, Inc., New York & London
1971

Introduction

World War I proved a bitter jolt for a generation faced with a major conflict after a century of relative world peace. *This was especially true in England, where major social and economic reforms had accompanied the gradual extension of voting rights and where a strong trade union movement continued to apply pressure for still greater strides towards democracy. To some Englishmen the war, with its demand for total mobilization, meant an inevitable retrogression in the struggle for democratic government. Conscription became a symbol of the shift towards total obedience. For a people who prided themselves on their enlightened view of civil liberties, the idea of conscription was anathema. When it came most Englishmen complied with its odious requirements, but there was a minority who refused. Spearheading the English anti-conscription movement was the No-Conscription Fellowship, an organization originally created to defeat England's first conscription bill. Failing in that, it became the focal point of resistance to the idea of forced military service. The Fellowship, with its record of personal nonviolent resistance, provided a basis for the development of a much more ambitious and widespread antiwar movement in the post-war period. It was a major factor in the emergence of the first modern, international war resistance movement predicated on the idea that wars could not take place if individuals refused to fight. The post-war No More War Movement was a direct outgrowth of the No-Conscription Fellowship; the War Resisters' International and other antiwar organizations of the 1920's were influenced by its earlier efforts.*

W. J. Chamberlain was a key figure in the founding and work of the No-Conscription Fellowship. A member of the National Committee of the Fellowship and an editor of its Journal, The Tribunal, *Chamberlain was court-martialed four times and served a prison sentence for his opposition to the war. His book is both a first-hand account and a brief history of the Fellowship and its offspring, the No More War Movement, with its strategy of preventing war by collecting large numbers of pledges of refusal to participate in any future wars.*

In concise form W.J. Chamberlain describes the early efforts to stave off conscription and then the remarkable wartime underground operation of the Fellowship and its nearly uninterrupted publication of The Tribunal *in secret publishing places by courageous women editors who put out the paper when all the male editors were jailed. The Fellowship was composed of those who objected to both conscription and war. To its members only absolute exemption to the draft was acceptable. Any other form of alternative service they considered too direct an aid to the war effort for them to accept. These were men and women who insisted on recognition of their right, even during wartime, to live without killing. They kept alive the idea that the individual is more important than the state and that no emergency is so serious as to justify a denial of the very civil liberties that democratic governments claim they fight to protect. Some of their fellow countrymen who went to war found it much easier to understand and appreciate that idea than did officials, who viewed their stubborn disobedience with trepidation lest the love of personal liberty might indeed get out of hand.*

Lloyd George, the wartime prime minister who had himself opposed the earlier Boer War, showed no sympathy and even displayed overt intolerance toward the war resisters. High ranking military officials set out to break the objectors' spirits, sometimes resorting to brutal physical punishment or having them sent to France and then sentenced to death for disobeying orders. Civilian officials were equally lacking in understanding and on occasion unbelievably stupid, as when Archibald Bodkin, the Treasury Counsel (government prosecutor), summed up the position of the war resisters so well that they reprinted his words on a poster and displayed it all over England.

It was also shortsighted for officials to assume that punishing the resisters would break the movement. The government was dealing with men who took the ideals of democracy seriously. Their crime was not treason but rather that they loved their country too well. They were stubborn men with deeply-held convictions. Some had a religious basis for their objection but many more were socialists whose vision of a just society precluded the taking of life. In their opposition to war they related it to militarism, of which conscription was the cornerstone. By living example they proved that military might was incapable of converting individuals to a particular set of ideas. Ten of the jailed English resisters died in prison and sixty-three died later as a result of their ordeal, while others lost their reason. But the movement did not die out and in the years after the war it flourished on a scale previously unknown.

Chamberlain's book is most useful for the personal touch it offers to the early war resistance story. Some of the comments could only be added by a participant, and a few of them are especially poignant. Perhaps the most moving incident described is the death of an Irish Catholic resister, Paul Gillan, who took the ethics of Jesus seriously and who objected to fighting "for the country that had treated Ireland worse than Germany had treated Belgium." After court-martial Gillan refused to work in prison and the punishment of restricted diet and solitary confinement for ten months completely broke his health. When he was transferred to the same prison hospital where Chamberlain was confined he was already too sick to recover. Shortly afterward he "got his

INTRODUCTION

discharge" by death, as the author so fittingly described it.

W. J. Chamberlain recorded his version of the early antiwar movement in 1928 when the international peace movement was flourishing and people all over the world rejoiced over the many signatories to the Kellogg Pact which promised to outlaw war. Eleven years later the world was plunged into the most devastating war in history with its preview in Hiroshima and Nagasaki of future nuclear terror. The numerous super-power confrontations, the wars and terrorism in the Middle East, the spread of nuclear weaponry and the limited but highly dangerous conflicts in Korea and Southeast Asia all illustrate the continuation of war as an instrument of national policy. Nations still act on the delusive assumption that military preparations provide security against war.

It was opposition to militarism and conscription for which the World War I resisters sacrificed their freedom and sometimes their lives. Since then many others around the world have carried on the tradition of resistance. United States participation in war in Indochina has evoked more widespread and varied war resistance activity than ever before seen. Yet the military ideals persist; as this is written conscription is still a policy in the United States. A reading of W. J. Chamberlain's account of the World War I resistance can lead to despair and frustration over the continued influence of the military way, or it can encourage and *inspire young men to continue the struggle which began so long ago. Hopefully, it will tend to do the latter, for discouraging as the story of the struggle against war may seem, it would be disastrous to abandon the cause. Our hope for a more creative human environment, perhaps our hope for the future itself, depends largely on continued resistance to military control of our lives, for without such control, governments would have to give up war itself.*

Larry Gara
Wilmington College

FIGHTING FOR PEACE

Fighting for Peace

THE STORY OF THE WAR RESISTANCE MOVEMENT

By

W. J. CHAMBERLAIN

with a FOREWORD by
HAROLD J. MORLAND, M.A.

Published by the
NO MORE WAR MOVEMENT
11 Doughty Street, London, W.C.1

" The historic epochs that men are most eager to keep in living and inspiring memory, are the epochs where ' the mind that is man ' approved itself unconquerable by force."

—LORD MORLEY

AUTHOR'S NOTE.

THIS book has been written at the request of the National Committee of the No More War Movement, and in response to a desire that the thousands of young men and women who are opposing all war may know something of the early history of the Movement. Many of those now in the Movement were at school during the Great War ; many others got their knowledge of the stand made against that war from the "patriotic" Press of those days. It is for such as these that this book is primarily intended ; but it may be that those who took part in the struggle will read with interest this story of the events which played such a big part in their lives.

The story has been told in greater detail by John William Graham in his book, *Conscription and Conscience*, published in 1922 by Allen & Unwin, Ltd. Much that was in that book will of necessity be found in these pages ; but the movement has grown to a remarkable extent since 1922, and even those who read John William Graham's book will find much that will be new to them.

W.J.C.

CONTENTS

13

ILLUSTRATIONS

15

FOREWORD.

THE greatest condemnation of war is not the
sacrifice of human life in its prime, nor yet the
irreparable damage, both physical and moral, to
a much larger number of those who take part in it,
still less the waste of material resources which
might be used, under wise guidance, to redeem
our civilisation. Any one of these taken singly
should be reason enough for putting an end to
such a monstrous outrage, but taken in combina-
tion these visible consequences are less finally
unbearable than the hidden results arising from
the way in which war overrides and sets at naught
the primary demand of the free spirit of man to be
allowed to work out its own salvation in accord-
ance with the inner urge which we call conscience.

There was a time when war was for those who
liked it ; bands of mercenaries hired themselves to
the highest bidder, regardless of nationality and
with no pretence of a righteous cause. Modern
war is a more serious affair and cannot be carried
out on a large scale without compulsion. In
peace-time the army can be recruited from the

failures in the industrial struggle and officered by men who make it their profession as others choose the Law or the Church. But in time of war (fortunately for one's faith in human nature) men must be herded and driven into the army, and their natural repugnance is branded as "cowardice."

The essential vice of conscription is not that it necessitates the persecution of those who are determined not to yield to it, but that it breaks down the decent reluctance of the much greater number who have never thought of opposing the commands of constituted authority. The real injury is done to those who are compelled into the army while those who resist and are merely "deemed" to be soldiers (save for some tragic casualties) come out of the struggle with a new mastery of themselves and of life.

None of the men and women, who are the heroes of this graphic history, regretted any suffering that came their way. They followed the Light that led them on, and the things that happened to them were merely incidents. The title "Fighting for Peace" is a happy description of their state of spiritual activity. They were not

18

content to be passive resisters, and as a matter of
fact, in guard-room, police-court and prison they
made many converts to their cause. Their
object was not to secure personal exemption
from war service, but to make war impossible.
Thus the efforts to secure their release from
prison were not stimulated or in the main
approved by them ; and in particular the
Society of Friends refused any exclusive exemption and refrained almost to the last from joining
in the appeals for release which arose spon-
taneously from the public conscience.

It has not been easy for Will Chamberlain to
write this story, as he was all the time in the
thick of the battle, but his readers will be the
more grateful to him for the simple record, and
will not be deceived by the absence of heroics into
overlooking the real heroism that underlies it.
It is easier for me to pen the Foreword as I was
always on the fringe of the fight. In the early
years of the war, I was above the conscription age,
and later on, when the age was raised, I was by no
choice of my own in a sheltered occupation and
never called up ; but as relative, personal friend,
or Quaker chaplain, I knew and honoured many

of those whose story is here told. They were men and women of all types and descriptions, alike only in this characteristic, that they were not prepared to surrender the citadel of their soul. "Conchies," yes, and for that very reason the salt of the earth.

They blazed the trail to be followed by the No More War Movement and the War Resisters' International, which aim at making war impossible by organising those who refuse to take part in it and are prepared to work for an order of human life in which it can find no place. The Tribunals which gave or withheld exemptions during the war were not always very understanding in their criticisms of the conscientious objector, but there was some basis for their suggestion that objection to war should originate in peace-time. Most of those who fought for peace in war-time are acting as recruiting agents for this new army, which is constituted on a voluntary basis and will in time carry all before it.

" Now is the Time." Mr. Ponsonby's 130,000 signatures are evidence of the existence of a great public opinion hostile to war, but the imagination of the peoples needs to be captured by the idea of a warless world as within the reach of the rising generation. We should welcome every indication of increased co-operation and of the breaking down of the barriers between nations. We should be willing to co-operate with anyone who cherishes the ideal of peace. Leagues and Pacts play an important part in improving international relations and making war less likely, but war will only become impossible in so far as men and women refuse to take any part in it. *Si vis pacem, para pacem.*

HAROLD J. MORLAND.

October, 1928.

THE VISION.

FIGHTING FOR PEACE

CHAPTER I.

WHEN EUROPE WENT MAD.

A T midnight on that tragic Fourth of August, 1914, the present writer stood at the window of a little hotel in Bristol and listened to a great crowd cheering and singing "Rule, Britannia" and "God Save the King." The newspaper offices had just posted up the fatal news :

" WAR DECLARED ! "

At first there was a hush as the printed sheet was displayed. Then somebody raised a cheer, which was taken up by the crowd ; and soon everybody in the street was mad with the war fever.

The fever was still at its height at the breakfast table next morning. Everybody talked about the war and its strategy.

"It will be all over by Christmas . . . ."
"We shall march straight to Berlin. . . ."
"Too big to last more than a few months. . . ."
"Time the Germans were taught a lesson. . . ."

Thus they talked ; a stout commercial traveller, an elderly man with the air of a retired colonel, a couple of farmers, and the proprietor of the hotel. There was also an elderly lady with white hair and a sad face. She broke into the general conversation.

"*I hope they will not take my boy*," was her contribution.

* * * *

The weeks went by, and the young men flocked to the colours, fired by a great and generous impulse. They believed that "Gallant little Belgium" had been invaded ruthlessly by the Germans. Press, Pulpit and Platform lured them on. "Scrap of paper . . ." "Barbarous Huns . . ." "War to end War . . ." "Make the World safe for Democracy . . ." Trusting, believing, they enlisted in their thousands ; left the desk and the bench and donned the uniform in the belief that they were helping to rid the world of war.

They were not told then, what Mr. Lloyd George told us after the war, that the country had "stumbled blindly" in the war. Nor were they told what we know now, that the war was "inevitable" because secret diplomacy had made it so, and that Great Britain was committed to France by an agreement of which the British people knew nothing, and the existence of which was denied by the British Prime Minister in the House of Commons a few days before the outbreak of war.

The months went by, and there was no more talk about it being "all over by Christmas." The papers began to talk about "digging in," about "all the resources of the nation" being required to achieve victory. The response of the young men was "magnificent," but it was "not enough." An army of millions would be required to defeat the hordes of men in field-grey uniforms who were entrenched so dangerously near

26

Paris and the coast. Conscription was openly advocated in some of the "powerful articles" which began to appear in the daily and weekly papers.

*   *   *   *

It was a woman Socialist and Pacifist who sounded the call to the War Resisters. Lilla Brockway, wife of A. Fenner Brockway, was the first to feel that the time had come to gather together all those in the Socialist and other movements who would refuse to be driven to the murder of their fellows if conscription came. At her suggestion, her husband wrote a letter, which appeared in the *Labour Leader* (now the *New Leader*) towards the end of 1914, asking all who were determined not to fight to send their names to Lilla Brockway, so that common action might be taken if and when conscription came.

In response to that call there came replies from every part of the country—from little fishing villages in Cornwall and from far north of Scotland ; from agricultural districts as well as from the big cities came letters which showed that not everybody had succumbed to the madness of war. The greater part of the replies were from members of the Independent Labour Party ; among the rest were members of the Society of Friends, and a few were from members of other religious bodies.

In her home at Marple, Lilla Brockway collected the names in a file, and she and her husband waited for the time when that handful of young men would be called upon to resist the State's demand that they should take up arms. They did not have long to wait. The call for more and more cannon-fodder made it obvious that conscription would come. Early in 1915 it was decided to form the No-Conscription Fellowship, and a Provisional Committee, consisting of Fenner Brockway, Clifford Allen, J. H. Hudson, and the Rev. Leyton Richards held several meetings to decide how best to organise resistance to conscription. Lilla Brockway did most of the secretarial work in those early days, but it was soon found necessary to appoint a full-time secretary, and open an office in London. Aylmer Rose was the first secretary, and an office was opened at Merton House, Salisbury Court, off Fleet Street.

In July, 1915, it was decided to take steps to create a network of Fellowship branches all over the country and the present writer was asked to undertake this work. A few weeks later, when the Compulsory Registration Act had become law, Fenner Brockway, Lilla Brockway and I spent most of a week-end going through the names of those who had responded to the letter in the *Labour Leader*.

Our aim was to convene a conference of delegates from all parts of the country for the following November, and tell the Government plainly that conscription would be resisted by thousands of young men who believed that war was murder and would refuse to take part in it, whatever the consequences. Up to that moment the War Resisters' movement was little more than a collection of names and addresses in a file. By October, 1915, branches had been organised in fifty centres throughout the country, and it was decided to hold a national conference at the Memorial Hall, Farringdon Street, London, on November 27th, in the knowledge that the Conscription

Bill would be introduced in the House of Commons a few weeks later. Branches were being formed right up to the day of the conference. There were sixty-one branches represented at that first conference of the No-Conscription Fellowship, and delegates came from as far afield as Cornwall and Glasgow. The Plymouth branch was formed a day before the conference, and a delegate was sent to London from the inaugural meeting.

That conference was the beginning of the Fight for Peace : it was the first move in what was destined to become a great world-wide revolt against the insanity of war. On that day a handful of young men threw out a challenge to the most powerful Government of modern times and stood for the right of every individual conscience to decide whether a man should take part in that organised and legalised mass murder we call war.

29

CHAPTER II.

THE MEN WHO STOOD AGAINST WAR.

BEFORE dealing with the conference proceedings and their outcome, it may be well to anticipate the query that must be in the minds of many readers : What manner of men were those who refused to respond to the country's call in the Great War ?

If the jingo Press references to them during that period of insanity were reliable guides, most of those young men were either cranks or cowards. The *Daily Express* dubbed them "pasty faces" ; to the general public they were just "conchies" —a term first used, I believe, by a parson !

Let us consider first the leaders of the movement, not because they were more important than the rank and file, but because they were more in the public eye at the time. The following persons constituted the National Committee of the No-Conscription Fellowship at the time of its first conference : Clifford Allen (chairman), Edward Grubb (hon. treasurer), A. Fenner Brockway (hon. secretary), W. J. Chamberlain (hon. organiser), Walter H. Ayles, A. Barratt Brown, John P. Fletcher, Morgan Jones, C. H. Norman, Rev. Leyton Richards.

Clifford Allen was a brilliant young Socialist who, after leaving Cambridge University, had thrown himself into the work of the Labour movement, and was general manager of the *Daily Citizen* up to the time that paper ceased publication.

Frail in body, but strong in spirit, and with a magnetic personality which endeared him to all who came in contact with him, he was an ideal leader of the movement. He professed no religion other than his Socialism.

Edward Grubb, M.A., was a well-known member of the Society of Friends, who, although too old to be called upon to fight, felt it to be his duty to give his whole-hearted support to the young men who, irrespective of religious or political views, were taking the stand against war which Quakers had taken for over 200 years.

Fenner Brockway, the son of a missionary, was a young Socialist journalist who became editor of the *Labour Leader* after serving for some years on the staff of the *Christian Commonwealth*—a Christian Socialist weekly journal which made a feature of the sermons of the Rev. R. J. Campbell at the time the "New Theology" was being preached from the City Temple. Two years ago Brockway was reappointed editor of the *New Leader* in succession to H. N. Brailsford. Before entering journalism, he was a social Settlement worker in Pentonville. Like Allen, he professed no religion other than his Socialism.

W. J. Chamberlain was a journalist and a Socialist, who left Capitalist journalism to join the staff of the *Daily Citizen*. At the outbreak of the war, his "religion" was a mixture of Socialism and Tolstoyism. He joined the Society of Friends while in prison and is still a member.

Walter H. Ayles was also a Socialist, and a prominent leader of that movement in Bristol, as well as a member of the

National Council of the I.L.P. He was for some time Labour M.P. for Bristol North. He joined the Society of Friends while in prison, and is now Organising Secretary of the No More War Movement.

A. Barratt Brown, B.A., was a young Quaker, of Woodbrooke Settlement, Bournville, Birmingham. He was also a member of the I.L.P., and is now Principal of Ruskin College, Oxford.

John P. Fletcher was another Quaker of military age, who had experience of conscription in Australia, and was formerly secretary of the Australian Freedom League.

Morgan Jones was a Welsh teacher and a well-known Socialist leader in South Wales. After the war he had the distinction of being the first Conscientious Objector to be elected to Parliament, defeating a Coalition and a Communist candidate by a huge majority.

C. H. Norman was a shorthand writer in the Law Courts, and a member of the I.L.P., holding strong anti-militarist views.

The Rev. Leyton Richards was a Congregational minister, who had to leave his Church at Liverpool because he insisted upon preaching Christianity in war-time. He is now the Pastor of Carr's Lane Church, Birmingham.

With the exception of Edward Grubb and the Rev. Leyton Richards, all the members of the National Committee were liable to be called up under the Conscription Act, and Clifford Allen, Fenner Brockway, W. J. Chamberlain, Walter Ayles, J. P. Fletcher, Morgan Jones, and C. H. Norman were among those who were refused exemption and resisted conscription. A. Barratt Brown was granted exemption by a Birmingham Tribunal, but the exemption was withdrawn later on the application of the military authorities—much to Barratt Brown's relief !

As the members of the original National Committee were removed to prison, others stepped into their places.* They represented all shades of political and religious opinion. Many were outstanding figures in their professions. All were united in their conscientious objection to war. Among the thousands who resisted conscription, were arrested, court-martialled, and sent to prison, were doctors, teachers, well-known Quaker social workers, journalists, etc., as well as agricultural workers from-remote villages. Men from the Universities joined hands with men from the fields, factories, and workshops in this great stand for the sanctity of human personality. Liberal Quakers and Socialists stood side by side with men who had nothing in common with them except a hatred of war and a determination not to take part in it.

* The following served on the Committee at one time or another :—
J. H. Hudson (now Labour M.P. for Huddersfield), Henry Davies (South Wales), James Marshall, Francis Meynell, James Maxton (now M.P. and Chairman of the I.L.P.), Ernest E. Hunter, Catherine E. Marshall, the Hon. Bertrand Russell, James Crawshaw, Dr. Alfred Salter (now M.P.), Ada Salter, Joan M. Fry, Sutherland Campbell, Percy Redfern, Theodora Wilson Wilson, B. J. Boothroyd, Neil Maclean, M.P., Alexander C. Wilson, Mrs. Lees, Tom Snowden, J. Austin, Marion Daunt, Violet Tillard, Mrs. Goodwin, Rev. G. S. Woods, C. Scrymgeour (now M.P.), Hugh Gibbins, Nora Gibbins, J. Theodore Harris, Isaac Goss, A. W. Brunt, Henry Bolton, H. P. Bell, H. T. Turland, and John Winning.

Stephen Hobhouse (eldest son of the Right Hon. Henry Hobhouse), a scholar of Eton and Balliol, who had renounced his position and prospects as his father's heir, joined the Society of Friends, and devoted his life to social work in the East End (actually sharing the poverty of the people among whom he worked), could have secured exemption on medical grounds, but he refused to be medically examined, and took his stand with the rest of the men who went to prison.

T. Corder Catchpool was a Quaker who joined the Friends' Ambulance Unit in 1914, and worked with the Unit in the hottest of the Ypres battles. While at the front he found that the Unit was being used to displace men who were drafted into the firing line, so he resigned and came back to England to take his stand with those who were resisting conscription. He was sent to prison in the usual course, and while in prison was awarded the Mons Medal for his service in Flanders !

Hugh Gibbins, a well-known Quaker business man in Birmingham, who was also a member of the I.L.P. and a keen worker in the Adult School movement, would have been allowed by the Tribunal to continue his business if he would accept such an exemption, but he refused to recognise the authority of the Tribunal, and was sent to prison and remained there until the end of the war.

Wilfred Wellock (now Labour M.P. for the Stourbridge Division) was a member of a religious body similar to the Quakers, possessing no paid ministry. This body made an arrangement with the War Office whereby all the preachers on its plan (and Wellock was one) could receive complete exemption by applying for it. But Wellock refused to take

34

advantage of this way of escape, holding the view that the exemption of ministers was a class privilege and unjustifiable.

Dr. Ernest B. Ludlam, a master at Clifton College, was engaged in scientific experiments at Cambridge when he was arrested for refusing to respond to the call under the Military Service Act. The Government offered him exemption on condition that he continued his research work. But when he found that his successful experiments were being used for military purposes, he refused to continue his work, was arrested, and sent to prison.

Malcolm Sparkes was the man who founded the Builders' Parliament and devised the plan which formed the basis of the Whitley Councils. His business was taken under the control of the Government for war purposes, and he resigned his directorship and was soon among the War Resisters in prison.

Maurice L. Rowntree (son of the late Joshua Rowntree) another Quaker social worker, was among these who went to prison ; and many other men in humbler walks of life made every sacrifice it was possible to make for the cause of peace, short of laying down their lives. Some there were who made that sacrifice, and of these we shall write later.

In this brief story of the War Resisters' movement it is not possible to do more than give a bare indication of the character of the men who took part in it. There may have been among the thousands who joined the No-Conscription Fellowship in those days a few who had no higher motive than that of evading military service ; but they were very few, and none of them stood the test when confronted with the alternative of imprisonment. If there were such men, their lot was made easy by the various offers of alternative service. By this I do not mean that the acceptance of alternative service was proof that the person accepting it had not a genuine objection to war —many accepted alternative service because they felt that the State, having recognised their conscientious objection to fighting, had a right to demand some form of service in war-time. But it is obvious that if a man wanted nothing more than to "save his skin," the Government made it easier for him than for the man who felt that any kind of service imposed by the State in war time was as the Tribunals put it, "of national importance," and therefore calculated to assist in the prosecution of the war. To these men there was no choice other than to refuse such service and suffer the penalty of indefinite terms of imprisonment. And without desiring to belittle the stand taken by those who accepted one or the other forms of alternative service (some of whom suffered much at the hands of the military, or in prison, before they took this step), it must be stated as a fact that those who refused it and went to prison made their position easier to understand by the men in the trenches—besides creating the most difficult problem for the Government. This aspect of the fight for peace is dealt with more fully in a later chapter.

CHAPTER III.

The Basis of the War Resisters' Movement.

Now let us see just what the No-Conscription Fellowship stood for. The basis of the Fellowship was thus set out in its Constitution :—

> "The No-Conscription Fellowship is an organisation of men likely to be called upon to undertake military service in the event of conscription, who will refuse from conscientious motives to bear arms, because they consider human life to be sacred, and cannot, therefore, assume the responsibility of inflicting death. They deny the right of Governments to say, ' You shall bear arms,' and will oppose every effort to introduce compulsory military service into Great Britain. Should such efforts be successful, they will, whatever the consequences may be, obey their conscientious convictions rather than the commands of Governments."

All who joined the Fellowship in its earlier days fully accepted the above basis, but as the movement grew, it was found that there were men who, while utterly opposed to war, had certain reservations on the question of the sanctity of human life. The Fellowship admitted them because it was realised that it would be impossible to allow a man to struggle alone when he was conscientiously opposed to war, but might hold the view that in certain exceptional circumstances it may be necessary to take human life.

The most concise explanation of the movement was contained in the chairman's address delivered by Clifford Allen at the first conference at the Memorial Hall, on November 27th, 1915. The essential parts of that address are worth quoting in full :—

"As soon as the danger of Conscription became imminent, and the Fellowship something more than an informal gathering, it was necessary for those responsible to consider what should be the basis upon which the organisation should be built. The conscription controversy has been waged by many people who, by reason of age or sex, would never be subjected to the provisions of the Conscription Act. The chief characteristic of this Fellowship is that full membership is strictly confined to those men who would be subject to the provisions of any such Act. . . .

"Having decided that we must have some common basis of belief, we had to look round in order to discover which one of the objections to conscription was that which met with general approval among our members, and so should form the basis of our organisation. Upon examination we discovered the following objections to conscription: There were first the groups of people who strongly advocated war, but who differed as to whether the best way of carrying on war was the voluntary or the conscript system . . . In addition to this argument, we discovered others that were being advanced: arguments that conscription would be the gravest possible interference with individual liberty in this country of free traditions ; that conscription would be a menace to the development of the Trade Union movement ; that, indeed, the imposition of conscription might be construed as the first step towards its inevitable conclusion, the domination of the military caste and the military spirit in Britain.

"We examined all these views, and, after careful discussion, we unanimously rejected the whole of the first group, which may be described as merely military or strategic. So far as the second group of opinions was concerned, those dealing with the infringement of individual liberty, and with the danger to the Trade Union movement, it was immediately apparent that each of us held very firmly one or all those opinions—that, in fact, our objection to conscription was intensified just in so far as we held vigorously one or all those views. But that was not all. We discovered a fact, which is the most important characteristic of our organisation, that not only did we individually hold such views as I have expressed, but that there was one objection to conscription which we shared with intense fervour, and that was a belief in the sanctity of human life. *The members of the No-Conscription Fellowship base their fundamental objection to conscription on this ground : that whatever else a State may or may not do, whatever infringement of individual liberty a State may or may not effect, there is one interference with individual judgment that no State in the world has any sanction to tamper with—that is, to tamper with the unfettered free right of every man to decide for himself the issue of life and death.*

"*We contend that the individual conscience alone must decide whether a man will sacrifice his own life or inflict death upon other people in time of war, and that however far the State may impose its commands upon the will of the community, the right of*

39

private judgment in this particular must be left to the individual,
since human personality is a thing which must be held as sacred.
Upon that we have built our organisation. It is because we hold
that view so intensely, whilst believing in the other arguments that
I have indicated, that nothing would ever induce us to betray our
deep religious and moral conviction by accepting conscription."

Thus did Clifford Allen state the faith that was in those
young men, all of whom knew that within the next few months
they would be called upon to put their faith to the test. The
conference was most impressive. There was no spirit of
boastfulness : only a quiet, dignified determination that, come
what may, no power on earth would compel them to do a
thing which they believed to be wrong. Towards the end of
his address, Allen said calmly but deliberately :—

"If, despite our present determined opposition, and
notwithstanding our determined opposition in the future,
conscription becomes the law of the land, we are willing to
undergo the penalties that the State may inflict—yes, and even
death itself—rather than go back upon our convictions. Let
it be clearly understood that the members of our organisation
have not formed the Fellowship in order to shelter themselves
from suffering. . . . May we not say with perfect truth that
just in proportion as we men have to suffer for the cause of
Peace we shall advance that cause ; and just in so far as we
cause the Government to persecute those who believe in
Peace, so we may be doing the greatest service which has been
performed since the war broke out to stimulate the national
conscience in that direction. Probably far more powerful
propaganda than countless meetings, or countless declarations,

will be the testimony of men who are willing to suffer rather than sacrifice their convictions in this matter of Peace."

At the conclusion of Allen's address, the following declaration was made unanimously, the delegates standing in silence:

"That we, the delegates and members of the No-Conscription Fellowship assembled in national conference, fully conscious of the attempt that may be made to impose conscription on this country, recognising that such a system must destroy the sanctity of human life, betray the free traditions of our country and hinder its social and industrial emancipation, though realising the grave consequences to ourselves that may follow our decision, hereby solemnly and sincerely reaffirm our intention to resist conscription, whatever the penalties may be."

From that memorable gathering the delegates went back to their homes in all parts of the country to carry on an energetic campaign against conscription. The first Military Service Bill was introduced in the House of Commons by the late Lord Oxford (then Mr. Asquith, and Prime Minister of the first Coalition Government) on January 5th, 1916. Prior to its introduction, the Fellowship, with the whole-hearted support of the Society of Friends, the I.L.P., and a number of Socialist and Pacifist M.P.s, conducted a vigorous anti-conscription campaign throughout the country. It was realised that once the Bill became law, all opposition to conscription would be illegal, and the campaign was therefore the more intense because of the shortness of time. But it was obvious from the outset that the military authorities were determined to have conscription ; and when, in spite of the opposition, the Bill was known to be drafted ready for presentation, influence was brought to bear on Mr. Asquith so that a clause was inserted in the Bill giving the Tribunals power to grant exemption to those having "a conscientious objection to the undertaking of combatant service." Needless to say, the Bill gave no instructions to the Tribunals as to how they were to discover whether a man had a conscientious objection. The clause went on to state :—

"Any certificate of exemption may be absolute, conditional, or temporary, as the authority by whom it is granted think best suited to the case, and also, in the case of exemption on conscientious grounds, may take the form of an exemption from combatant service only, or may be conditional on the applicant being engaged on some work which in the opinion of the Tribunal dealing with the case is of national importance."

To the credit of Mr. Asquith, it must be recorded that in spite of the jeers of a number of Tory M.P.s, he strongly defended the conscience exemption, but pointed out that it would only exempt men from combatant service. Among those who opposed the second reading of the Bill were Sir John Simon, Mr. Arnold Rowntree, Mr. Harvey, and many of the Labour M.P.s. During the committee stage, Mr. Philip Snowden moved a clause to safeguard the conscientious objector against the death penalty, pointing out that there was a danger of the extreme penalty being inflicted in the cases of men whom the Tribunals deemed not to have a conscientious objection. Sir F. E. Smith gave an undertaking that the death penalty would not be inflicted on such men, and the clause as finally passed excused the conscientious objector from the death penalty for refusing to obey the call to the colours.

It was afterwards held that this clause covered only the *first* refusal and rendered the persistent objector liable to the penalty after his forcible inclusion in the army! How loosely the clause was interpreted may be gathered from the fact that the death sentence was actually passed on a number of conscientious objectors who had been taken to France and court-martialled. Mr. Asquith was promptly made aware of this action of the military authorities, and only his intervention prevented the sentences being put into effect.

During the debates in the House there were some outstanding defences of conscientious objection—and some silly attacks on it. Mr. Joynson Hicks (now Sir William—popularly known as "Jix") called the conscience clause "the Slackers' Charter," and suggested that it should be confined to Quakers. But the Quakers had already made it known that they would not accept such an exemption. Among the notable speeches made in defence of the conscience clause (apart from those made by the Quaker M.P.s and the Labour M.P.s) was that of Mr. Herbert Samuel, then Home Secretary. "Is it really contemplated," he said, "that now, when for the first time you are making military service compulsory in this country, it should be accompanied by the arrest and imprisonment of a certain number of men who unquestionably, by common consent, are men of the highest character, and in other matters, good citizens ? "

The full story of the gallant but hopeless fight against the Bill by a handful of Quaker, Socialist, and Liberal Pacifist

43

M.P.s is told in John William Graham's *Conscription and Conscience*. All that need be added here is that only thirty-eight Members voted against the third reading, and it became law after Lord Courtney of Penwith had put in a great plea, in the House of Lords, for a broadening of the conscience clause to make it include a conscientious objection "to undertake any service or engage in any action in support of the war or to the undertaking of combatant service." The Bishop of London was among those who opposed this amendment, and it was not accepted by the Government. The first Conscription Act became operative on March 2nd, 1916.

A PRISON CELL, LOOKING TOWARDS
THE HEAVILY-BARRED WINDOW.

Drawing by E. M. Wilson.

45

CHAPTER IV.

The Persecution Begins.

The setting up of Tribunals under the Act left members of the Fellowship no option other than to appeal for exemption on the grounds of conscientious objection. There were many who felt that even this seeming concession should not be made, but the majority view was that every opportunity should be given to the Government to do the right thing. The first application had to be made to the local Tribunal; there were also Appeal Tribunals, and a Central Tribunal. But as was only to be expected, in the great majority of cases the proceedings of the Tribunals were farcical. As John William Graham has said, the task of the Tribunals in dealing with conscientious objectors, was "the most extraordinary attempt to exercise spiritual insight ever handed over to bodies of amateurs." The members of the Tribunals were in the main selected from people who had been active on recruiting platforms. Even in the few cases—and they were very few—where the Tribunals were composed of fair-minded people honestly trying to carry out the expressed intention of the Government, their task was an impossible one.

Looking back on those days, one can still smile at some of the absurdities perpetrated by the Tribunals. This book could be filled with true stories of these absurdities, but there is room only for a few typical cases.

At a Midland Tribunal a Christadelphian,who appealed as a conscientious objector, was told by the chairman : "It is such people as you who are the cause of all wars. If I had my way I should try to abolish you Christadelphians."

At another Midland Tribunal a member suggested that a conscientious objector ought to be willing to do mine-sweeping —and then went on to explain that mine-sweeping meant sweeping out coal-mines !

At Sutton (Surrey) the military representative at the Tribunal was the local vicar, who protested strongly against every claim made on the ground of conscientious objection.

At Ellesmere a bricklayer based his objection on the teaching of Christ, and said if the nation had acted on Christian teaching there would have been no war. To which the chairman of the Tribunal replied : "Don't you really think that is a piece of humbug ? "

At Nairn the chairman of the Tribunal told a conscientious objector that the Bible told him to fight the Devil, and added : "If the German Emperor is not worse than the Devil, I am a Dutchman."

At Gower Tribunal its military representative told a conscientious objector that he "was only fit to be on the point of a German bayonet."

At Oxford Tribunal the military representative thought Tolstoy was the name of a place !

There were times when the military representative got more than he bargained for. Such an occasion was provided by Walter Ayles when he appeared before the Bristol Tribunal on

48

June 25th, 1926. Ayles was then a City Councillor, and he called the military representative (Colonel Burgess) as a witness on his behalf! The following interesting cross-examination took place :—

Walter Ayles : "I desire to ask you this question : Supposing I enlisted in the army, and was on Home Garrison Duty, and was captured with my wife and child and other comrades, and supposing the German threatened to tear my wife and child limb from limb if I refused to divulge military secrets concerning the docks and the channel which I had in my possession as a member of the Docks Committee. What would be my duty as a soldier ? "

Colonel Burgess (hesitating greatly)—

The Chairman : "The question is so hypothetical."

Colonel Burgess : "Yes, I agree it is very hypothetical."

Walter Ayles : "It's by no means hypothetical if our opponents are right. It has actually happened that men have had secrets involving the lives of others which they have refused to give up. However, let me ask the Colonel two more questions of a practical nature. Supposing I were a soldier, and was ordered, as one of a squad to shoot a condemned man. Would I have to do it ?"

Colonel Burgess : "Certainly."

Walter Ayles : "Even if I knew he was innocent ? "

Colonel Burgess : "Certainly, you must obey orders."

Walter Ayles : "My last question is this. Suppose I enlisted, and was sent with my regiment to a strike area, where my comrades were out on strike, and I was ordered to shoot

49

down my Trade Union comrades on strike. Would I have to shoot them ? "

Colonel Burgess : "Certainly."

All over the country men who appealed for exemption on conscience grounds were scoffed at, bullied, grossly insulted— and refused exemption. The treatment of such applicants soon became a public scandal. On March 29th, 1916, the *Daily Chronicle* made a strong protest against the scandal, in a leading article, in the course of which it declared that "every Tribunal being a law unto itself, some remarkable doctrines are laid down." Decent-minded public men wrote letters of protest to the Press, some of which were published, as, for instance, the following, written by Dr. Moore Ede :—

"Mr. Asquith, on whose word we are all accustomed to rely, promised that conscientious objectors should be exempted from military service. This exemption was embodied in the Act, and faith should be kept with the conscientious objector. The Tribunals are, of course, bound to see that the plea is not put forth as an excuse for shirking military service ; but when members of Tribunals, sometimes men notoriously irreligious, attempt to argue as to the teaching of the New Testament, there is something worse than a travesty of justice."

Among other ministers who made similar protests was the Bishop of Oxford, who wrote as follows to *The Times*, on March 16th, 1916 :—

"Sir,—I do not hold the views of those who are seeking exemption from military service on grounds of conscientious objection to war under any circumstances. I can quite believe (though I have no evidence of it) that some of those who take this stand may really be shirkers. But I know one or two men personally (not members of the Church of England) who, I am sure, are not shirkers, men whom you might accuse of fanaticism, but never of cowardice or stupidity. I think these men have not been treated by the Tribunals with sufficient respect. I feel sure that they will be driven to passive resistance, and that, whatever punishment is finally meted out to them, they will take it gladly. But ten cases of punishment for conscience's sake would establish their cause with very many who are deaf to their reasonings."

The Free Church Council, through its General Committee, also passed a resolution protesting against the injustices of the Tribunals. Even *The Solicitors' Journal* was moved to protest in a leading article which declared that "many members of Tribunals decline to recognise that there can be any conscientious objection to participation in warfare, and they have attempted to browbeat applicants in the style of the seventeenth century."

A letter of protest was also sent to the Press over the signatures of the following ministers of religion and other prominent men :—D. S. Cairns, G. Campbell Morgan, John Clifford, A. Clutton Brock, J. Monro Gibson, R. F. Horton, A. Mansbridge, C. Oxon, W. B. Selbie, W. Tenter, and Edward Winton.

The scandal was brought to the notice of the Government by Philip Snowden and other M.P.s, and so great was the volume of protest from representative people in all parts of the country, that Mr. Walter Long, on behalf of the Government, promised to remedy the injustices by giving special instructions to the Appeal Tribunals to go into all appeals carefully. But in spite of this promise, the situation grew worse instead of better. The Appeal Tribunals, instead of removing the injustices, added to them : in many cases applicants who had secured exemption from combatant service when appearing before the local Tribunals, had their exemptions removed by the Appeal Tribunals. A typical instance of the "justice" meted out by the Appeal Tribunals was that of a young Unitarian, who was granted exemption from combatant service and recommended for non-combatant service by the local Tribunal. He appealed to the London County Appeal Tribunal for absolute exemption, and produced proof of his anti-war views being held while at college before the war broke out. The Appeal Tribunal took away the exemption granted by the local Tribunal and ordered him to combatant service. This Appeal Tribunal adopted the same course with a young lay preacher in charge of the Gospel Lifeboat Mission at Peckham. Many Appeal Tribunals went so far as to declare that they had no power to grant absolute exemption to conscientious objectors. The most amazing instance of the attitude adopted by the Appeal Tribunals was at Durham, where the chairman declared : "We are not bound by any statement made by Members of Parliament, or any circular issued by the Local Government Board." !

"He cannot claim to be a Socialist and a conscientious objector," was another bright gem from a member of a Tribunal at Burnley.

"Short shrift was given by Nottingham Tribunal to several conscientious objectors to military service, whose claims for exemption were disallowed." That was how the *Birmingham Post* reported the proceedings of the Nottingham Tribunal on April 3rd, 1916, and it was a correct report of the proceedings of Tribunals all over the country.

For sheer blasphemy the following incident at the Clowne Tribunal will take some beating :—

Chairman, to conscientious objector : "Have you read where He went into the temple with a whip and lashed them out ? "

Applicant : "But He did not kill them."

Chairman : "No, but He probably would have done if He had had a gun."

Here is another bright specimen of the mental calibre of the Tribunals. The chairman of the Willesden Tribunal said to a conscientious objector : "Did not Jesus Christ say that we are to render unto Caesar the things that are Caesar's ? "

Applicant : "I do not consider that my conscience belongs to Caesar. Jesus also said, ' Ye cannot serve two masters.' "

Chairman : "But I say you *can* serve two masters ! "

At Shaw (Lancashire) a member of a Tribunal told a conscientious objector : "You are nothing but a shivering mass of unwholesome fat ! "

And so one could go on with this story of the insults and abuse heaped upon young men who were availing themselves of the legal right to apply for exemption. Prominent people of all shades of opinion were filled with disgust at the treatment these men were receiving ; and in addition to the protests mentioned above, the following significant letter appeared in the correspondence columns of *The Nation* in April of that year :—

"Sir,—I should be glad if you would publish these few words of a wounded soldier, if only to remove the widespread belief that those who are fighting have no respect for the conscientious objector. Just as, for the most part, those who volunteered to fight did so from a supreme sense of duty, so also do the conscientious objectors carry out what they consider to be their supreme duty to humanity and to their country. . . . The volunteer is honoured because he obeys the mandates of his conscience rather than the dictates of expediency. Why, then, should we persecute the conscientious objector for adopting precisely the same attitude ? '

The letter was signed by a soldier in one of the first regiments to suffer casualties in the war. A little later, when thousands of men who had been refused exemption were arrested, hauled before the magistrates, and handed over to the military authorities, the rank and file of the Army—and not a few officers—were more tolerant, and even sympathetic, towards the War Resisters than the stay-at-home members of Tribunals were. In a very few cases there was a certain amount of horseplay in the barracks and camps, due, it was afterwards discovered, to instructions issued by bullying officers to the effect that this kind of thing would soon break down resistance to military service. But immediately the No-Conscription Fellowship got to hear of these isolated cases, effective steps were taken to put a stop to them, and it can be said by the great majority of those who were "deemed" to be soldiers but steadfastly resisted all attempts to make them such, that the "Tommies" were their best friends. The present writer was court-martialled four times, and still remembers with gratitude many acts of kindness done to him by the soldiers with whom he came in contact during his periods of waiting in the guard-rooms of four different regiments.

By May Day, 1916, the records of the No-Conscription Fellowship contained the names of 102 men who had been arrested after being refused exemption, handed over to the military authorities, court-martialled for refusing to obey military orders, and sentenced to terms of imprisonment varying from twenty-eight days' detention to two years' hard labour. At that time arrests of War Resisters were taking place at the rate of about twenty per day. By the end of May nearly 700 men were in the hands of the military authorities, and several thousand more were passing through the hands of the Tribunals. Commenting on this fact, *The Morning Post* said :—

"The conscientious objectors have broken down the machinery of the Act, and there are enough hearings put down to last out a hundred years' war."

CHAPTER V.

D.O.R.A. at Work !

THE energetic campaign waged by the No-Conscription Fellowship soon attracted the attention of the jingo Press. From March, 1916, right up to the end of the struggle, the Fellowship issued a small weekly paper, *The Tribunal*. In the columns of *The Tribunal* Clifford Allen wrote cheering articles week by week, and the paper also contained all the news about the struggle, together with effective Pacifist propaganda, some of which enraged the pen-and-ink warriors of Fleet Street, who quoted extracts from the more striking bits of propaganda and called upon the Government to put a stop to this "treason and mutiny," as the *Daily Sketch* called it in an article demanding that the Government should "proclaim the Fellowship an illegal association, prohibit all its meetings and all similar meetings, and suppress *The Tribunal* and all similar publications." As a parting shot the indignant writer added :—

"Finally, and above all, they should consider as a matter of urgency what should be done with Allen, Brockway, and the rest of the gang."

On March 12th, 1916, the Government acted on this advice. In addition to publishing *The Tribunal*, the National Committee of the Fellowship had published a leaflet, immediately after the Conscription Act became law. In order to show the full extent of the "crime" committed by the leaders of the War

Resisters' movement, it is necessary to reproduce this leaflet in full. It read as follows :—

REPEAL THE ACT !

Fellow Citizens,—Conscription is now law in this country of free traditions. Our hard-won liberties have been violated. Conscription means the desecration of principles that we have long held dear ; it involves the subordination of civil liberties to military dictation ; it imperils the freedom of individual conscience, and establishes in our midst that militarism which menaces all social progress and divides the people of all nations.

We reaffirm our determined resistance to all that is established by the Act.

We cannot assist in warfare. War, which to us is wrong, war, which the peoples do not seek, will only be made impossible when men who so believe remain steadfast to their convictions.

Conscience, it is true, has been recognised by the Act, but it has been placed at the mercy of Tribunals. We are prepared to answer for our faith before any Tribunal, but we cannot accept any exemption that would compel those who hate war to kill by proxy or set them to tasks which would help in the furtherance of war.

We strongly condemn the monstrous assumption by Parliament that a man is "deemed" to be bound by an oath that he has never taken, and forced under an authority he will never acknowledge to perform acts which outrage his deepest convictons.

It is true that the present Act applies only to a small section of the community, but a great tradition has been sacrificed. Already there is a clamour for the extension of the Act. Admit the principle, and who can stay the march of militarism ?

Repeal the Act. That is the only safeguard.

If this be not done, militarism will fasten its iron grip upon our national life and institutions. There will be imposed upon us the very system which our statesmen affirm that they set out to overthrow.

What shall it profit the nation if it shall win the war and lose its own soul ?

The leaflet was signed by Clifford Allen, Edward Grubb, Fenner Brockway, W. J. Chamberlain, W. H. Ayles, A. Barratt Brown, J. P. Fletcher, Morgan Jones, C. H. Norman, and the Rev. Leyton Richards.

There was a big demand for this leaflet, and 750,000 were distributed throughout the country. When all but a dozen had been distributed, the Government decided to set to work to stop the distribution, and on the afternoon of March 12th, C.I.D. officers arrived at the offices of the Fellowship with a large van and a summons for every member of the National Committee, except Allen and Norman, to appear at the Mansion House Police Court a few days later to answer a charge under the Defence of the Realm Act. The omission of C. H. Norman from the charge was explained by the fact that he was already in the hands of the military authorities. But Allen was not "handed over" until some time after the case was heard, and nobody ever solved the mystery of his name being overlooked when the summonses were issued. The possibility is that the authorities thought he had been arrested under the Military Service Act weeks before his arrest took place.

The prosecution was "featured" in every paper in the country. One London paper (*The Daily Express*) threw overboard all the care which papers usually exercise in dealing with a prosecution before the case has been before the Court, and came out on the day after the summonses were received with a front-page article headed "Pasty Faces Summoned."

Far from being annoyed by this little politeness, the "pasty faces" rejoiced in the fact that the paper also reprinted the

58

offending leaflet in full, thus helping in the circulation of anti-Conscription propaganda.

The case was tried on May 17th, at the Mansion House, before Sir A. Newton. The counsel for the prosecution was Mr. (now Sir) Archibald Bodkin, K.C., Public Prosecutor. Mr. Harold Morris, K.C., defended. The charge was that the defendants had "made statements likely to prejudice the discipline and recruiting of His Majesty's Forces." The little Court was uncomfortably crowded with members and supporters of the No-Conscription Fellowship, and the eight defendants were even more uncomfortably crowded in the dock. Mr. Bodkin, comically pompous, took more pains than he need have done in presenting the case for the prosecution ; for the decision of the magistrate was never in doubt. But Mr. Bodkin thought it necessary to call Lord Derby (then Director-General of Recruiting) to give his opinion that the leaflet was likely to prejudice recruiting. The other "star" witness for the prosecution was Brigadier-General E. W. Childs, who was at that time "Director of Personal Service" at the War Office. He had the distasteful job of dealing with cases of courts-martial on War Resisters, and of course he had no hesitation in declaring that the statements in the leaflet were "entirely subversive."

A notable feature of the trial was the brilliant defence put up by Mr. Harold Morris, K.C. (who, by the way, had secured a commission in the Army and left to join the fighting service on the following day). He made a fine plea for liberty to express opinion even in war-time, and also made a big point of the assurance given by Mr. Herbert Samuel in the House of

Commons before the Act was passed, that "meetings which are limited to opposition to the passage of the Military Service Bill or to advocating its repeal, if passed, or opposition to any extension of compulsory service, and writings of the same character, would not be liable to suppression." Incidentally, he touched on the fact that some of the defendants were Quakers whose opposition to all war was a well-known part of their religious belief, and in cross-examining Brigadier-General Childs he asked that gentleman : "Do you know any Quakers ? "

"I am happy to say that I do not ! " was the reply ; and Mr. Morris sat down without another word to the Brigadier-General.

Among those who went into the witness-box was Mr. Edward Grubb, whose testimony to his Pacifist faith was given with impressive dignity and sincerity. In the course of cross-examination by Mr. Bodkin, he was asked to define his attitude towards non-combatant service—the offer of which by the Government was regarded as meeting the objections of War Resisters.

"If I would not kill another," said Mr Grubb, quietly, "I would not sharpen the knife for another person to do the killing."

Mr. Bodkin did not ask any more questions, but sat down with a look on his face which said plainly, "These people are beyond me."

The Rev. Leyton Richards was another difficult man in the witness-box. Clifford Allen's description of him was very apt. "While Fenner Brockway was in the box," said Allen, re-calling the trial, "he was like a careful batsman, watching the prosecution bowler very closely and guarding against being bowled out. But Leyton Richards hit out vigorously left and right, and scored with every hit ! " It was amusing to hear the Public Prosecutor quoting Scripture to Leyton Richards, and to hear Leyton Richards retort, "Yes, well, go on and complete the verse." But Mr. Bodkin never accepted the challenge !

The magistrate listened to the case with obvious impatience, and at the end, without a moment's hesitation, announced that he had come to the conclusion that the leaflet would prejudice recruiting, and that he must inflict the maximum penalty of £100 on each defendant, with £10 cost, or 61 days' imprison-ment as an alternative. Notice of appeal was given, and the appeal was heard a few weeks later, but was, of course, dismissed. Mr. Grubb, reluctantly, and for personal reasons (among which were the delicate state of his wife's health and the strong feeling of his friends, that his advanced years would not stand the strain of imprisonment) paid the fine. The Rev. Leyton Richards also paid his fine because he felt that he ought to accept the form of punishment meted out by the State. Fenner Brockway, W. J. Chamberlain, Walter H. Ayles, A. Barratt Brown, and John Fletcher went to prison for 61 days. (Morgan Jones was arrested under the Military Service Act and "handed over" to the military authorities before the appeal was heard.)

Looking back on the effect of that attempt to suppress opinion, one marvels at the stupidity of those responsible for the attempt ; for it resulted in nation-wide publicity being given to the very views which the Government were anxious to suppress. I have before me as I write, the Press cuttings giving accounts of the prosecution. The London and provincial papers devoted columns to the case, and every report contained quotations from the offending leaflet. Thus the original circulation of these "seditious" views was extended until it covered every newspaper reader in Great Britain. Another result of the prosecution was to provide the War Resisters with an effective piece of War Resistance propaganda from no less an authority than Mr. Archibald Bodkin, who, in his speech for the prosecution, declared :

"I submit, sir, that war would become impossible if all men were to hold the view that war is wrong."

That statement was published by the Fellowship in poster form and displayed all over the country—and several persons afterwards found themselves in the Courts for displaying it ! By that curious "reasoning" which prevails in war-time, the statement by the Public Prosecutor was first an argument against War Resistance and then an argument against recruiting !

When the members of the National Committee of the Fellowship went to prison, their places were at once taken by a "shadow" committee chosen as soon as it was realised that all members of military age were liable to "removal." This precaution was taken in the case of everybody who had any work to do in connection with the Fellowship, so that no matter who was taken, the work was carried on without dislocation ; and when all the men of military age were "removed," the women stepped into the breach, led by Miss Catherine Marshall.

But at this stage of the struggle it was felt that in the event of Clifford Allen being taken while the rest of the original National Committee were serving the 61 days' imprisonment, arrangements were to be made to secure the release of Fenner Brockway, by paying his fine, so that he could act as Chairman until he was taken under the Act. Allen was arrested after only a few of the 61 days had been served, and Miss Marshall went to Pentonville, paid Brockway's fine, and hauled him out of prison late in the evening. When the chief warder of Pentonville went to Brockway's cell and told him he was to be released, Fenner said "Damn ! " to the astonishment of the prison officials, who had never known a discharged prisoner receive the announcement of his release in such an astounding manner !

As an indication of the effect of the prosecution on the minds of those who, while supporting the war, were still hoping that the country might be spared the inevitable subordination of every semblance of liberty to the militarist spirit, the following extracts from the *Manchester Guardian's* comments on the case may be quoted :

"The police-court in the Mansion House, one of the smallest and least accessible of courts of justice, a sort of annexe to the Lord Mayor's apartments, was oddly chosen to-day as the scene of an examination of conscience. The alderman on his seat underneath the Lord Mayor's sword of state had before him, instead of the normal petty thefts, domestic squabbles, and morning-after-the-revels business, one of the most abstruse, delicate, and insoluble of problems— the position of the conscientious objector. In the little crowd behind the barrier, in place of the normal adherents of people meanly in trouble, one saw idealists and friends of unpopular causes and militants of the minority.

"At last the Government had decided to come to serious grips with the movement, which, as everybody knows, is supported by the people who cannot for a moment be dismissed by the facile label of anti-patriotism, and which gains its momentum from a conviction that safeguards deliberately placed in an Act of Parliament are proving insufficient to protect a sentiment which is as old as the history of English liberty.

"The No-Conscriptionist leaders were convicted and heavily fined for their leaflet, in which they carry on their warfare against the Military Service Act. No other issue could have been expected, but one felt, after the case, that the whole controversy has only been forced into a new and more painful phase. One could not but feel the futility of the discussions in which counsel, magistrate, and No-Conscriptionists were fumbling for a formula which would explain an intangible reality. The most astonishing thing said during the day was the remark of a highly-placed War Office official when asked if he knew any Quakers. He replied, 'I am happy to say I do not.' "

The *New York Evening Post* commented as follows on the prosecution :—

"To such lengths has the war passion carried England that she is now moving legally against a state of mind. To parallel such a persecution one must go back to the days of William Penn. This Fellowship is to-day the true exponent of the liberty of conscience of which the British have always been so proud. When the Defence of the Realm Act was passed, sober and responsible men like Lord Loreburn pointed out that it undermined the very foundations of the Englishman's rights for which he has been so jealous. These prophecies have come true. The law is literally covering a multitude of Government sins against personal liberty and conscience. Of course the No-Conscription Fellowship knows the risk it is running. It has been careful not to urge men to refrain from enlisting ; it has merely been an association for mutual support and encouragement in standing at any cost for a moral ideal, and as such it deserves applause the world over."

But that was written before America entered the war. Once America was smitten with the war fever the War Resisters in that country suffered the same persecution as they did in every other belligerent country.

The prosecution of the National Committee was followed by swift action all over the country against other members of the Fellowship. On June 5th, the Hon. Bertrand Russell, whose fame throughout the world as a brilliant mathematician and philosopher did not save him from the wrath of the "patriots" when he threw himself heart and soul into the work of the Fellowship (he became Acting Chairman when Brockway was arrested), wrote a leaflet setting out the bare facts of the treatment of Mr. E. Everett, a teacher of St. Helens, who was refused exemption by the Tribunal in spite of his well-known opposition to all war. This case was typical of thousands, but the position of Mr. Everett was such a strong one that Bertrand Russell felt that a statement of his case would influence fair-minded people. Immediately the leaflet was distributed, members of the Fellowship in various parts of the country were prosecuted under D.O.R.A. for distributing it. Bertrand Russell therefore wrote a letter to the *Times* pointing out that, as author of the leaflet, he was responsible and should be dealt with instead of those who did the distributing.

The Public Prosecutor acted promptly on this suggestion, and Bertrand Russell was prosecuted and fined £100. But again this prosecution served the cause of peace, for it secured publicity for a noble defence of Conscience by Bertrand Russell. He conducted his own defence, and his speech was frequently interrupted by the Lord Mayor who tried the case. In the course of his speech he said :

"The struggle to secure liberty for those who think it wrong to fight is now at its height. All who know the history of human freedom can recognise in this contest all the familiar features of the old struggle for liberty by which intolerance has been defeated in the past. . . . Whether I am acquitted or convicted matters little ; it is not I who am in the dock, but the whole traditional liberty which our ancestors built up through centuries of struggle and sacrifice. Other nations may surpass us in other respects, but that tradition has been the supreme good that we in this country have preserved more than anything else, and for that liberty of the individual I stand. I think that under the stress of fear the authorities have some- what forgotten that ancient tradition, and I think the fear is unworthy, and the tyranny which is resulting will be disas- trous if it is not resisted. I would say to them, ' You cannot defeat such men ———.' "

Here Bertrand Russell was pulled up by the Lord Mayor, and told that he was making a "political speech." The concluding portion of the speech, which the Lord Mayor refused to hear, was as follows :—

"The persecution which conscientious objectors have endured has enormously increased their moral weight. It illustrates the invincible power of that better way of passive resistance which pacifists believe to be stronger than all the armies and navies in the world. Men inspired by faith and freed from the domination of fear are unconquerable. The noblest thing in a man is the spiritual force which enables him to stand firm against the whole world in obedience to a sense of right ; and I will never acquiesce in silence while men in whom spiritual force is strong are treated as a danger to the com- munity rather than as its most precious heritage. I would say to the persecutors, 'You cannot defeat such men; you cannot make their testimony of no avail. For every one whom you silence by force a hundred will be moved to carry on his work, until at last you yourselves will be won over, and will recog- nise, with a sense of liberation from bondage that all the material force the world contains is powerless against the spirit of indomitable love."

67

Bertrand Russell was dismissed from his post at Cambridge University because of his activity in the War Resisters' movement, and he was not allowed to fulfil lecturing engagements in America. He was again prosecuted at a later date for an article he wrote in *The Tribunal*, and was sentenced to six months' imprisonment in the First Division.

On the day that Bertrand Russell was convicted, the head office of the Fellowship was raided by a force of police and stripped of all its documents and literature. The raid was made by order of the "competent military authority" under the powers conferred by D.O.R.A. But the work of the Fellowship went on just the same. When the police vans left the office, steps were taken to secure the duplicate copies of all the documents, files, etc., necessary to the work of the organisation, which had been deposited in a secret place in preparation for this emergency. All through the struggle against "competent" military authorities, the Fellowship organisation remained intact. In various secret places, buried in an orchard in Surrey, or locked in an unsuspected city merchant's safe, or at the back of the bookshelf in the house of a remote sympathiser who could take no open part in the work of the Fellowship, there were duplicates of every document likely to be seized; at no time during the struggle did the Fellowship lose touch with its members in guard-room or prison. Indeed, the Fellowship could, and did, supply information to the War Office about young men who had been handed over to the military and lost so far as the War Office records were concerned. It was not a rare occurrence for Catherine Marshall to be rung up by Brigadier-General Childs's department and asked for information about certain War Resisters whose parents had written to the War Office !

All through this persecution the women of the movement were splendid. If one mentions only a few of the more outstanding names, it is not because the work of the thousands of women in all parts of the country was of less value than that performed by those at the head of the movement, but because in such limited space one can only hope to give an impression of the wonderful way in which the women in the Peace movement rallied behind the men and helped them to endure to the end. There was never a word other than of encouragement from the women who visited their men-folk in prison. In spite of the fact that for most of the families of the imprisoned men there was a hard struggle to live—a struggle that was eased to some extent by the organisation of a measure of financial relief to such families—and the equally hard task of bearing patiently the sneers and insults that were heaped upon all connected with the despised "Conchies," the women went to the prison visiting rooms and smiled cheerfully at their men through the two wire-netted screens that separated them.

The name that comes first to my mind is that of Violet Tillard—and a lump comes in my throat as I see her ever-cheery face through the mist. She had been a militant suffragette, and came into the No-Conscription Fellowship in its early days, first in connection with the maintenance organisation, and, later, became General Secretary when Aylmer Rose was arrested. She served 61 days imprisonment for refusing to divulge to the police the name of the printer who was secretly printing *The Tribunal*. She remained with the Fellowship until all the men were released from prison. Then she went to Russia to assist in Quaker relief work in the famine areas. There the dread typhoid caught her, and she died as she always wished to die—in the service of humanity.

Mention of the cause of Violet Tillard's imprisonment leads one to the memory of Joan Beauchamp's amazing achievement in keeping *The Tribunal* running with all the best brains of the C.I.D. vainly trying to find out where it was being printed. Joan stepped into the breach as publisher of the paper after first the present writer, and then B. J. Boothroyd (now better known as "Yaffle" of the *New Leader*— if I may be pardoned giving him away !) were removed from the Editorial chair by the military authorities. The paper was originally printed by the National Labour Press, but that works was raided by the police and the machinery dismantled. Then a comrade in the movement, S. H. Street, undertook to print the paper, and did so until his plant was smashed up by the police.

Scotland Yard was jubilant. "We have done for you this time ! " said a C.I.D. officer to Lydia Smith, who was in charge of the Press Department, and was editing the paper at this time. But *The Tribunal* appeared as usual the next week ! It had been printed in a small hand press in a secret place which Scotland Yard never discovered. Joan Beauchamp, whose imprint appeared on the paper every week, was arrested and fined £100 or 51 days' imprisonment. But when the appeal was heard it was found that the publisher could only be fined for each copy "so printed by her," and as the prosecution could not prove that she had printed a single copy—indeed, the prosecution admitted that much—there was an *impasse*. The result in the end was a sentence of imprisonment, but Joan was released after serving ten days. She had previously served a month's imprisonment for printing an article by Bertrand Russell to which the authorities objected.

The funniest story of this episode is that told about a young lad who had been employed to convey *The Tribunal* from the secret press to the office of the Fellowship. One day the bundle proved too heavy for him, and he left it on the Embankment in charge of a policeman while he went to the office for help ! The policeman never suspected the nature of his charge, and the secret press remained a secret.

Catherine Marshall was another woman who threw herself heart and soul into the work of the movement. She had attended the first convention as a fraternal delegate from the Women's International League, and was so impressed by it that she decided to devote her whole service to the movement. When the work of the Fellowship grew so large that it had to remove to bigger offices in the Adelphi, Catherine Marshall established a Record Department, where the history of every War Resister was recorded and which was the source of much valuable propaganda material. She was also in charge of the Political Department, and in a hundred and one ways was of tremendous value to the movement.

Ada Salter (wife of Dr. Alfred Salter, M.P.) rendered great service while in charge of the Maintenance Department Gladys Rinder, in her work on the Information Bureau, was largely responsible for the amount of support secured for the various protests to the Government. Edith Ellis, who was Acting Secretary of the Friends' Service Committee, and who was one of the members of that body to serve six months' imprisonment for publishing a Quaker Peace leaflet without first submitting it to the Censor, co-operated whole-heartedly with the Fellowship in all its work, and, when the War Resisters were released from prison, converted her home at Wray Head, near Scarborough, into a convalescent home for them.

The War Resisters' movement owes much to the women in all walks of life who rallied to the cause of Peace in the days when the rest of the world was worshipping at the bloody altar of the God of War. A tribute must also be paid to the Society of Friends, which, alone among the religious bodies, threw all its resources into the movement; and to the Independent Labour Party whose whole-hearted support enabled the movement to make its voice heard in Parliament.

A PRISON CELL, SHOWING IRON DOOR,
WITH SPY HOLE.

Drawing by E. M. Wilson.

CHAPTER VI.

"EVEN UNTO THE GATES OF DEATH."

BY June, 1916, over 800 members of the Fellowship were in the hands of the military authorities, and were being court-martialled for refusing to obey military orders. The whole business was thoroughly disliked by most of the officers in the Army, who, after the attempt to break the spirits of the resisters had failed, realised that the effect of the courts-martial was far more calculated to influence the rank and file of the Army in favour of the resisters than against them. Every barracks and military camp in the country had War Resisters in the guard-room. The proceedings leading up to the courts-martial were in most cases farcical from the point of view of impressing the ordinary soldier with the all-powerful discipline of the Army. A War Resister would arrive in camp from the police-court under military escort. In some cases he would be allowed the run of the camp for a day or two on giving his word not to attempt to get away ; in other cases he would be put in the guard-room on arrival to await the opportunity to commit the "crime" of disobeying a military order.

The next move was the arrival of a major or a captain, accompanied by a couple of sergeants, one of whom carried a uniform : "You are Private John Smith ? " said the superior officer. "My name is John Smith" was the usual reply. The officer would grunt a little and then order the Resister to don the uniform. "I am sorry, but I must respectfully refuse," the Resister would reply. The order would be repeated, only to receive the same reply. Then followed the court-martial and the inevitable sentence of two years' hard labour. In the early days the local Press published fairly full accounts of the courts-martial, and in many cases the War Resisters were able to make effective pacifist statements in justification of their refusal to fight. Where a young man was able to make such a statement, it was listened to patiently by the officers of the court, and it is undoubtedly true that many members of His Majesty's Forces were impressed with the sincerity of the men whom they were compelled to send to prison.

The most extraordinary experience came my way while I was in the guard-room awaiting my first court-martial. One night the sergeant of the guard was astonished by the appearance at the guard-room door of a young man who announced that he had come to give himself up as a deserter. The man stammered a lot, and it was some time before he could make the sergeant understand what he was saying. When at last the sergeant understood, he said, "Don't be a —— fool ! You clear out, my lad, while the going's good ! "

But the man refused to go, and after more forceful but useless language from the sergeant, he was put in the guard-room for the night, and reported to the commanding officer next morning. With great difficulty he managed to convince the commanding officer that he had deserted from a certain regiment, and was remanded for enquiries. It took nearly a week for the military authorities to verify the man's story, and then he was put down for trial on the charge of deserting from the army.

My journalistic instinct was aroused, and I got the whole story from the man, painfully it is true. It was, briefly, that he and his brother had enlisted in the early days of the war, had been drafted to a camp on Salisbury Plain, and while there had been bullied by a certain drill sergeant. The brother stood it, but this man could not, and so, one night, he walked out of the camp and did not return. He got a job as a munition worker (using an assumed name), and his brother went to the front— and was killed.

The death of his brother tortured the mind of the deserter day and night, and at last he could stand it no longer, and walked to the barracks to give himself up so that he could, as he said, "Go out and kill the —— German who killed my brother."

To cut a long story short, I felt that the man's story was such a human one that no court-martial would deal harshly with him if the whole case could be put properly. So I persuaded the man to apply for me as his "friend" to put his case at the trial. The application staggered the commanding officer, but as I knew that the Manual of Military Law provided for every prisoner having the right to be represented by a "court-martial friend" if required, and that even a fellow-prisoner was not barred from acting in that capacity, the request was granted.

We were given every facility to prepare the case. For several days we were solemnly marched, under armed escort, from the guard-room to the barracks library, where I wrote out a complete statement of the man's case and put in a plea that the charge should be altered to that of "being absent without leave." I appeared with him at the court-martial, and got the charge reduced according to my plea. Instead of being given a stiff sentence for desertion, he was sentenced to a few months' detention in barracks, during which he had to work at his own trade.

I never met him again, but I shall always remember how he tried to stammer out his thanks to me as we were being marched away from the court-martial—and the sensation it caused among the Tommies in the barracks when the result was known !

* * *

In an effort to appear reasonable, the Government decided to revise the sentences of two years to four months, hoping that four months in prison would make the Resisters see things in a more "reasonable" light. But this move merely increased the difficulties of the military authorities, for most of the men came out of prison more determined than ever ; and when they refused again and again to obey military orders, after serving first four months, then six months and longer, and knowing that their refusal would mean further imprisonment, the respect of the ordinary soldier increased, and many a War Resister was treated more as a V.C. hero than as a "coward" when he returned to the guard-room and persisted in his refusal of all military orders.

One of the things which outraged Mr. Bodkin's sense of decency when he was prosecuting the National Committee of the Fellowship was a headline in *The Tribunal*, "Preaching Pacifism in the Barracks ! " But that headline was a correct description of what was happening. It was inevitable that the Resisters should take every possible opportunity of explaining why they refused to fight, and in every guard-room there were attentive and in most cases, sympathetic audiences of soldiers. Here are typical extracts from letters written by Resisters from guard-rooms while awaiting court-martial :—

"I really wish you were here. It is one of the finest experiences I have ever had . . . Nearly every man we have come in contact with, even officers, are really sympathetic with us, and all they do to us they have to do because they are part of the machine. Many are eager to hear our views."

That was written by a young Quaker. Here is a letter from a young Socialist :—

"Just a line from a happy man who has been sentenced to two years' detention for remaining true to his principles of International Socialism. I feel that the time I have spent among the soldiers has not been in vain, as I have preached the gospel of Brotherhood and Internationalism to them whenever possible. On every occasion they have listened attentively, have asked many questions that troubled them, and at the conclusion have almost invariably said, ' You are quite right ; it would be a happier world if it could come about.' The pathetic way in which this has been said to me, both by young boys and men, has helped to make me more determined to suffer in the effort to save the curse of militarism from being shackled on the workers of this country. I go, therefore, to my confinement with a light heart and a smiling face, feeling that those who are persecuting us now will, in the near future, be dethroned and that International Brotherhood will one day triumph and permanent peace be secured."

Mr. Lloyd George, who was the Prime Minister most responsible for the persecution of War Resisters during the "War for Freedom," may be interested in the following extracts from a letter signed by a dozen young Welshmen in the guard-room at Cardiff :—

"Dear Chamberlain,—We hope to be able to smuggle this letter through. Escorted to this guard-room on Monday. No supper ; slept on floor without blankets. Tuesday morning, no breakfast. Taken to major and ordered to sign ration forms. Refused. Major threatened us with death penalty. . . . Disobeyed all orders. Still no food. Again asked to sign rations form and again refused. Victory at last ! Bread and cheese for supper ! Blankets ! Salmon for breakfast ! ! Soldiers now learning the ' Red Flag.' Whatever lies before us, we can face it. We have formed a branch of the Fellowship in the guard-room ! We have made many converts here. Later : Have been removed to separate cells."

Hundreds of such letters were received at the offices of the Fellowship. Most of them were smuggled out by sympathetic soldiers, who even went so far as to buy the stamps when the writers had no money or stamps.

As a contrast to this courteous and sympathetic attitude, which was fairly uniform in the treatment of Resisters in the hands of the military after the Fellowship had exposed the early cases of gross ill-treatment, and put a stop to them, it may be well to touch briefly on the experience of those who were the victims of the first reaction of the military authorities when faced with the problem of dealing with men who defied them. To be quite fair to the officers concerned, it has to be remembered that their knowledge of War Resisters was confined to what they had read about them in the "patriotic" Press. They thought they were dealing with "pasty faces," "shirkers," men who were out to "save their skins" at all costs, and in a few cases they acted as one would expect soldiers to act towards that kind of person. "Treat 'em rough!" was the order given to soldiers in charge of an early batch of Resisters, and the order was obeyed. On refusing to submit to military authority the resisters were kicked, reviled, stripped of their clothes and left to stand in their shirts for hours on end. I have no desire to stress this phase of persecution, because it quickly passed, but the fact must be recorded that some of those who were passed on to military authorities in the first few weeks of the struggle endured physical and mental torture of the vilest kind—and stood the test.

At Cleethorpes, a War Resister (James Brightmore) was put in a pit 3 feet by 2 feet, 12 feet deep, with 2 feet of water, and was kept there for four days. He was told by an officer that five of his companions had been sent to France and shot, and that he would be the next to suffer the same fate.

Another man (Jack Gray) was put into a sack, thrown into a pond eight times, and pulled out by a rope around his body.

The most outstanding instance of these early attempts to break down the resistance of the objectors was the despatch of a number of War Resisters to France, where, according to military law, they were liable to be shot for refusing to obey orders on active service. News of their arrival in France reached the Fellowship, and prompt steps were taken to raise the matter in Parliament. On May 9th, the day after they arrived in France, Mr. Asquith, who had not yet been ejected from the Premiership by Mr. Lloyd George, told Mr. Arnold Rowntree that he knew nothing about the matter. On the same day Professor Gilbert Murray, who had just returned from France, interviewed Lord Derby, then Secretary for War, and was told that the men would be shot "and quite right, too ! " if they persisted in their refusal to obey orders. Gilbert Murray was then able to get an interview with Mr. Asquith, who was obviously shocked by the news. "Abominable ! " he said, and gave an order to the Commander-in-Chief forbidding the executions without the knowledge of the Cabinet. But for Gilbert Murray's rush to Mr. Asquith, those men would have been shot.

A few weeks later, when definite intimation was given in Parliament, it was to the effect that thirty-four death sentences had been pronounced on War Resisters sent to France, and that the sentences had been commuted to ten years' penal servitude. From the ignorance of members of the Government when questioned in the House, it was obvious that they were practically helpless against the determination of the military authorities to break the spirit of these men. The despatch of the Resisters to France was in direct defiance of the pledges given by Ministers that men who refused to obey military orders on conscientious grounds would not be liable to the death penalty. While in military prisons in France these men were given severe punishments, including "crucifixion" (Field Punishment No. 1), which meant being hand-cuffed to the wheel of a gun-carriage for hours exposed to the sun and the flies. This form of punishment was so severe that it has since been abolished in the Army. Here is a description of "crucifixion" as it was endured by one of the men sentenced to death :—

"Each of us was placed with our backs to a framework consisting of uprights, at intervals of four yards, and cross-beams at a height of about four feet from the ground. Our ankles were tied together, and our arms then tied tightly at the wrists to the cross-beams ; and we had to remain in that position for two hours. The second evening we were placed with our faces to the barbed wire of a fence. As the ropes with which we were tied were fastened round the barbed wire instead of the usual thick wooden post, it was possible to tie them more tightly, and I found myself drawn so closely to the fence that when I wished to turn my head I had to do so very cautiously to avoid my face being torn by the barbs. To make matters less comfortable, it came on to rain and a bitterly cold wind blew across the top of the hill."

But those young men who suffered even to the extent of hearing their death sentences pronounced did not give in. One of them, on learning that he was to be court-martialled in France and that the death sentence was certain to result, wrote as follows :—

"My five comrades (there were six in his military prison) have reconsidered their position in the light of the latest information, *and all of us have decided to remain faithful even unto the gates of death.* For my part I am not depressed by my prospects. *I should consider it an honour to die for the cause.* I have been a soldier in the real fight for freedom all my thinking life, and although, judged by the perfect law, I am an unprofitable servant, I have sometimes been faithful, and I hope I shall not fail at the finish.

"I expect my comrades at liberty are agitated by the news of our probable fate, but I suggest that they do not devote all their efforts to procuring our release. Remember that the ideas of patriotism and militarism are surrounded with the glamour of self-sacrifice which the heroism of innumerable soldiers has cast upon them. Sacrifice hallows our cause. I suggest therefore, that you concentrate some of your thoughts in encouragement of the complete service to our ideal, so that when the final hour arrives we shall be nerved to endure, and then the principle of International Fraternity will be placed on an equal footing to the prejudice of patriotism."

Here is an extract from another letter describing the actual experience of being sentenced to death in France :—

"On the evening of Thursday, June 15th, the four of us who had been court-martialled were taken by an escort of military police to the Henriville Camp in order to hear our sentences read out. It was evidently intended to be an impressive function, as a large square consisting of the N.C.C. and Labour Battalions was drawn up on the parade ground. These men occupied three sides of the square, with a miscellaneous collection of spectators in the background, while we, with our escort, were placed on the remaining side. After a hum of conversation and comment had been suppressed by the N.C.O.s, I was marched out a few paces in advance of my

companions towards the centre of the square.   An officer . . .
read a long statement of my ' crimes ' and then announced the
sentence of the court : ' To suffer death by being shot.' . . .

"I have often been asked what my sensations were at that
moment, and I have found it difficult to recollect very clearly.
I think I may say that for the time being I had lost the sense of
' personality,' and, standing there on the parade ground, I had
a sense of representing something outside my own self,
supported by a greater strength than frail humanity.   However, in a few moments it was evident that the whole had not
been said, and the officer went on to say (after a pause) that
this sentence had been confirmed by the Commander-in-Chief
(another long pause), but afterwards commuted by him to one
of penal servitude for ten years."

And it was of these men—the "Absolutists," who would
take no part in war, neither in the fighting services nor in any
kind of alternative service, that Mr. Lloyd George said, in the
House of Commons on July 26th, 1916 :—

"I shall only consider the best means of making the path of
that class a very hard one."

But not all the war-time Ministers took that view.   In an
earlier debate (May 20th), Mr. Tennant, Under-Secretary for
War, had said :—

"I would like to say on my own behalf that, while the
conscientious objector has not made my path easier, and has
not eased the wheels of the chariot of war, and is not likely to
do so, I am afraid I cannot, for my part, withhold my—I do
not want to use too strong a word—but certainly my respect

for persons who on religious grounds will undergo privation and even persecution rather than do violence to their conscience. I would make that admission at once, and I hope the House will realise that that is my view."

All the men sentenced in France were sent back to England to serve their sentences in civil prisons.

THE MEN WHO WERE SENTENCED TO DEATH.

Name.	Town.
BARRITT, C.	Pinner.
BEAVIS, H. S.	Edmonton.
BONNER, B. M.	Luton.
BREWSTER, H. S.	Merton Park (London).
BROCKLESBY, J. H.	Rotherham.
CARTWRIGHT, C.	Leeds.
CRYER, E. C.	Cleveland.
EVANS, A. W.	Ilford.
FOISTER, J.	Cambridge.
GAUDIE, N.	East Bolton.
HALL, S.	Leeds.
HALL, C.	Leeds.
HICKS, G. E.	Burgess Hill (Sussex).
JACKSON, C. R.	Leeds.
JORDAN, P. B.	Little Milton (near Wallingford).
LAW, H. G.	Darlington.
LAW, W. E.	Darlington.
LOWN, R. A.	Stansford, Lincs.
MARTEN, H. C.	Pinner.
MARTLOWE, A.	York.
MURFIN, F.	Canonbury (London).
MYERS, A.	Cleveland.
PRIESTLY, A.	Stafford.
RENTON, L.	Leeds.
RICKETTS, O. G.	Petworth (Sussex).
RING, J. R.	W. Kilburn (London).
SCULLARD, H. W.	Sutton (Surrey).
STANTON, H. E.	Luton.
TAYLOR, A. W.	Edmonton.
WALLING, A. F.	Edmonton.

A QUAKER MEETING IN PRISON.

Drawn by S. Langford Jones
(from a rough sketch made in Pentonville Prison)

CHAPTER VII.

The Public Conscience Roused.

The greatest tragedy of war is its soul-destroying effect on the average decent citizen. Things against which all that is good and noble in the mass of the people would revolt in time of peace are allowed to be done in time of war under the plea, "We must do this thing, bad as it is, or we shall lose the war." But one claim can be made by those who stood out against the war in the teeth of persecution and unpopularity : they kept the real soul of the nation alive. It is true that its voice was weak and was for the most part drowned in the mad clamour of war, but however inaudible, it survived, and there were times when it was heard even above the boom of the guns and the cries of the warmongers.

The incidents related in the preceding chapter created a sensation in the House of Commons, and the more courageous among the leader-writers wrote strongly protesting articles. The *Daily News* said :—

"When questioned on Thursday night on the subject of the sentence of death passed on four conscientious objectors in France, Mr. Tennant said he had heard nothing about it, and declared that he believed it to be wholly untrue, and added that as the men were not in the face of the enemy they could not be treated as if they were. Yesterday Mr. Tennant had the humiliation of confessing that what he knew nothing about and did not believe on Thursday, was nevertheless more than true. Not four, but thirty-four men had been sentenced to death in circumstances which he said only a few days before could not possibly admit of that extreme course. We sympathise with Mr. Tennant. And we wonder what are the relations of the Army and the War Office which make it possible for a proceeding of this sort to take place and for the civil authority to be ignorant of the fact for nearly a week after the event. Where are we drifting ? "

The *Manchester Guardian* commented as follows on the incidents :—

"The final test of sincerity is the willingness to face consequences, and the supreme test the perseverance to death. The conscientious objector has been marked and flouted as a slacker and a coward. . . . Thirty-four conscientious objectors have carried their perseverance to the point of hearing a death sentence pronounced on them. The sentence has in no case been carried out, but if it has been commuted it is to a long term of penal servitude—ten years in most cases. We hope that people will now be satisfied that the conscientious objector may at least be what he professes to be, and is not necessarily a mere coward masquerading under a fine pretence. We hope that members of the Tribunals which sent these men into the Army may be stricken by some belated sense of shame."

Lord Courtney wrote to the *Times* :—

"To act upon the principle that it is right and necessary to punish the individual because in the highest conception of duty he withstands the world against him is to act upon the supreme maxim of Prussianism, which we all reject as the negation of morality."

But the strangest thing that happened at this period was the passing of what amounted to a vote of censure on the Government in the House of Lords ! On July 4th, Earl Russell called attention to the cases of brutal treatment of War Resisters in certain barracks, and mentioned in particular the case of Mr. C. N. Norman, who was given a very rough handling at Wandsworth Detention Barracks. (By the way, Norman was refused exemption by the Tribunal in spite of the fact that no less a person than Bernard Shaw appeared before the Tribunal and testified that he had known Norman's objection to war for many years prior to the outbreak of the Great War.)

Earl Russell moved :—

"That in the opinion of this House it is undesirable to subject military prisoners to punishments not authorised by law."

It was in this debate that the Government spokesman (Lord Sandhurst) announced the latest decision of the Government for dealing with War Resisters who were refused exemption by the Tribunal. It was to the effect that in future such men as refused to obey military orders would be sent to court-martial and would then be placed in civil prisons. Those who gave an undertaking to accept "work of national importance" would be released from prison and put on such work. Those who refused such work would complete their sentences of imprisonment and then be discharged from the Army. The final decision as to who would be adjudged "genuine" and offered alternative service would rest with the Central Tribunal.

After the Archbishop of Canterbury and Lord Devonport had expressed disappointment at the Government's reply to Earl Russell's charges, the motion was declared carried. It must be added that both the Archbishop and Lord Devonport were careful to disown any kind of sympathy with the views of the War Resisters.

Another significant happening was the refusal of the Fritchley (Derbyshire) Bench of magistrates to hand over to the military authorities a local Quaker who had been arrested after being refused exemption by the Tribunal. A York magistrate also refused to hand over a local Resister whom he declared to be genuine ; but in this case the Resister was brought before another Bench and handed over in the usual way.

* * *

The work of the No-Conscription Fellowship now became a definite and positive campaign for peace. Its earlier work was of necessity largely that of giving guidance to its members in the various phases of the struggle. From now onward it followed the policy outlined in the last message to members signed by the National Committee on the eve of the departure of most of its members to prison :—

"We conscientious objectors are not out to save our own souls and consciences any more than our own skins ; we are out to save the world from war. Conscience is not simply a private scruple which can be satisfied by withdrawal from the evil thing. It is a positive and compelling conviction which drives us to active work for the cause we have at heart. We are out for Peace—not the mere declaration of peace terms, nor the signing of peace treaties, but the creation of that state of mind and spirit which will make it impossible for nations to go to war."

The message went on to outline the various ways in which members of the Fellowship could work for the cause of peace through organisations such as the I.L.P., the Society of Friends, the Peace Negotiations Committee, and similar bodies. But above all, it stressed the fact that steadfastness to the principle of personal resistance was the greatest service that could be rendered to the cause of peace.

Meanwhile, the arrests of War Resisters and the prosecutions under the Defence of the Realm Act continued. One could fill pages with stories of the stupidities of the "competent" military authorities in their vain attempt to stem the tide of peace propaganda throughout the country. Among the many silly things done in D.O.R.A.'s name was to prohibit Bertrand Russell from entering certain prescribed areas which included most of the industrial centres. This petty action was taken because he was known to be delivering a series of lectures on philosophy in various parts of the country. He was thus prohibited from delivering a lecture in Glasgow, but Robert Smillie was allowed to read the lecture in the Glasgow hall! The result of the Government's persecution of Bertrand Russell was that he was dismissed from his lectureship at Trinity College, Cambridge.

Many advocates of peace in all parts of the country suffered similarly in the loss of appointments. Peace meetings were broken up just as they were in the worst periods of the Boer War, when Mr. Lloyd George was a War Resister instead of a persecutor of War Resisters. But the fight for peace went on all the time, although it was obvious that, as John Burns was alleged to have predicted, the war would be ended only by revolution in one of the belligerent countries, or by sheer exhaustion. Mr. Lloyd George had set his face against peace by negotiation and had declared for the "Knock-out blow." On seven occasions, beginning with the German offer of negotiations in December, 1916, and including the invitations by the Pope and President Wilson to the warring Powers to discuss peace terms, the Allied Powers shut the door on peace and thus paved the way for the disastrous "peace" which, in its economic results, proved almost as great a catastrophe as the war itself.

It was no easy thing to resist war in those dark days—to be one of a little band of men and women who stood by their peace principles while the rest of their fellows followed blindly at the heels of the war-mongers. But in prison cell and guard-room the fighters for peace were kept true to their faith by a sure belief in the ultimate triumph of their cause. In *The Tribunal* of November, 1916, Fenner Brockway gave expression to this belief in a prophetic message to his comrades :—

"We stand for an entirely New World after the war, for a world in which the peoples shall feel their unity so clearly that war will be unthinkable to them. Everyone of us has a part to play in building that New World. There must not be an idle member of the Fellowship if it is to be worthy of its principles.

After the war I hope to see the No-Conscription Fellowship linked up with uncompromising anti-militarist organisations in other parts of the world, so that in every land there may be organised bodies of men and women who will refuse in future to participate in war."

How that prophecy was fulfilled within a few years after it was made will be told in a later chapter.

* * *

Here we must leave the story of the arrests and imprisonment of these men. In all, 6,261 War Resisters were refused exemption by the Tribunals, arrested, handed over to the military, court-martialled, and sent to prison. In addition to these, there were nearly 5,000 men who accepted alternative service of various kinds, 3,300 who joined the Non-Combatant Corps, 1,200 who worked in the Friends' Ambulance Unit, and about 100 who joined the Royal Army Medical Corps.

So far as can be ascertained, just over 16,000 men refused to take up arms because of their conscientious objection to war. Of that number, about 1,500 refused every kind of alternative service and chose to remain in prison until released at the conclusion of the war, or until released because their health broke down. Nearly 900 served sentences of two years or more. Ten died in prison, and 63 died after release. Thirty-one lost their reason as the result of their experiences. The number of men given absolute exemption on grounds of conscience was not more than a dozen.

The imprisonment of so many men whose only "crime" was their refusal to take part in war had a profound effect on the

95

prison system in this country. When the first batch of War Resisters entered the prisons they were treated more severely than ordinary inmates. They were "jumped on" by prison officials for the slightest breach of the harsh prison rules— especially the silence rule—and were given extra punishment in the form of solitary confinement and bread-and-water diet. But a change very soon came over the prison officials, most of whom were ex-soldiers, and the harshness gave place to tolerance and in many cases acts of kindness which were forbidden by prison rules. And of course the War Resisters soon devised ways and means of breaking most of the inhuman rules without involving the officials in trouble. Elaborate (and often painful !) systems of carrying on "conversations," by the Morse code tapped on the walls of cells, and other methods, were adopted ; some chess enthusiasts were even able to plan a method of playing their favourite game by signals given from one cell window to another !

Prison "journals" were circulated in some prisons. Odd scraps of paper used for wrapping mail-bag rings were treasured, carefully wiped clean with a wet rag, dried flat between the pages of the Bible, and written on with stumps of pencil which most of the men managed to smuggle in, even though every man was stripped of all his clothes and had to go through a bath before donning the "broad arrow" prison suit. (I smuggled my pencil into prison by secreting it in my hair until I got to the cell, when it was usually possible to find a tiny hole in the wall ; others adopted the device of sticking a pencil to the soles of their feet with sticking plaster !)

After a time several minor concessions were made to War

Resisters in prison ; one could have a limited number of one's own books in one's cell, for instance. But no substantial difference was made between War Resisters and burglars or any other class of prisoner, except that the War Resisters were segregated from the others in most prisons. The event most looked forward to by many War Resisters in prison—apart from the visit of relatives—was the weekly service conducted by Quaker "chaplains," who were a great source of inspiration and encouragement.

The release of War Resisters set loose a great body of prison reformers who, from first-hand experience, could testify to the sheer inhumanity of the prison system. A great deal of evidence was placed before the Penal Reform League, but the most effective effort in this direction was the establishment, by the Labour Research Department, of a Prison System Enquiry Committee, of which Fenner Brockway and Stephen Hobhouse became joint secretaries. They collected a great mass of evidence from War Resisters who had been in every prison in the country, and the result was the publication of a report in book form, entitled *English Prisons To-day*. The exposures contained in that book, together with the practical reform advocated, were the chief cause of the noteworthy changes which have now been made in our prison system. This work has now been followed by a further book by Fenner Brockway, entitled *A New Way with Crime*, in which he advocates the total abolition of the prison system and outlines alternatives for the scientific treatment of crime. Let us hope that we may soon have a Home Secretary who will have the courage and imagination to put these proposals into operation.

THE MEN WHO DIED.

The following seventy-three War Resisters died after arrest, the first ten while in prison :—

BONE, WALTER	....	....	Birkenhead.
BRIDLE, O. S.	....	....	Brighton.
BURNS, W. E.	....	....	Failsworth.
BUTLER, A.	....	....	Stockport.
CAMPBELL, P.	....	....	Isle of Skye.
GILLAN, P. L.	....	....	London.
HORTON, A.	....	....	Manchester.
WILKINSON, F.	....	....	Dulwich.
WILSON, A.	....	....	Blackburn.
WINTER, J. G.	....	....	Cornsay.
ALLEN, PETER	....	....	Nelson.
ALLEN, TOM	....	....	Nelson.
ALLEN, WALTER G.		....	New Southgate.
BARLOW, A.	....	....	Mansfield Woodhouse.
BATTENHAM, F.	....	....	Downham Market.
BENYON, H.	....	....	Swansea.
BOWDEN, F.	....	....	Oldham.
BRENTNALL, A. G.	....	....	London.
BRIGHTMAN, H.	....	....	Camden Town.
CAINEY, THOMAS	....	....	Manchester.
CAMPBELL, N. A.	....	....	Glasgow.
COBB, C. J.	....	....	Croydon (o).
CROSBY, ERNEST	....	....	Liverpool (2).
DARDIS, G. H.	....	....	Risca.
DELLER, L.	....	....	West Brompton.
Dunbery, P.	....	....	Blackburn (1).
ENGLAND, E.	....	....	Leeds.
EUNGBLUT, A.	....	....	London, N.W. (12).
EVANS, J. LL.	....	...	Cardiff (3).
EVANS, R. G.	....	....	Reading.
FIRTH, H. W.	....	....	Norwich.

GOULDSBOROUGH, H.	Blackburn.
HALL, PERCY	Old Dalby.
HASTON, H.	Chesterfield.
HENDERSON, A.	Dundee.
HIRST, H. M.	Stalybridge.
HURST, A.	Southwark.
HOAD, H.	Chart Sutton.
HOOPER, R.	Bradford.
HURLEY, W.	Camberwell.
HURST, H.	Manchester.
JACKSON, THEODORE	—— (4).
JAMES, ALBERT L.	Kingston (5).
JAMES, H.	Worcester
LINSCOTT, S.	Newton Abbot (14).
MACLOLM, W. W.	Glasgow (6).
MARRIOTT-DODINGTON, S.	Hereford.
MARTLEWE, A.	York (7).
MATCHETT, T. D.	Bath.
MAY, W.	Edinburgh.
MOSS, —	Morley (8).
MOUNTFIELD, J.	Manchester.
PARKIN, W. H.	Sheffield.
PARTON, F. L.	Chiswick.
PEDDIESON, A.	Glasgow (14).
PHIPPS, H.	Harringay.
RICHMOND, ROYLE A.	Brighton (13).
RIGG, J. A.	Barrow-in-Furness.
ROBERTS, W. L.	Stockport.
RUDALL, A.	Newport.
SLATER, A. J.	Glasgow.
STAFFORD, N.	Hyde.
STANTON, W.	Leicester.
STATTON, —.	Cardiff.
SWETTENHAM, W.	Liverpool.
TAYLOR, J.	Silvertown (9).
THOMPSON, C.	Norwich (10).

TODD, G.	....	....	Willesden (11).
WALLIS, B.	....	....	Newmarket.
WHINNERAH, G.	....	....	Barrow-in-Furness.
WHILMORE, P. A.	....	....	Coventry.
WOODWARD, E.	....	....	Birmingham.
ZACHNIES, C.	....	....	Glasgow.

(0) A clerk by profession. Unpaid preacher and Sunday-school teacher. Served five terms ; three-and-a-half-years in prison. Released from Winchester in the last stage of consumption, and died three weeks later, March 17, 1919. He had also curvature of the spine, due to carrying coals at Pentonville for ten weeks.

(1) Died in the Military Hospital at Bangor, May, 1916.

(2) Removed from Wormwood Scrubs before the conclusion of his sentence, and died at Epsom, June, 1917.

(3) Contracted consumption during his imprisonment at Cardiff and detention at Newhaven Camp ; sent home from Wakefield in a dying condition and died at home, May, 1917. A clerk and student for the Baptist ministry.

(4) Died in Clipstone Camp, December 14th, 1916.

(5) Died of consumption at Wakefield, May 17th, 1917, due to the cold at Wormwood Scrubs.

(6) Released on furlough from camp and died at home, June, 1917.

(7) Sentenced to death in France, June, 1916. Worked under the Home Office scheme at Dyce ; left it on September 12th, 1917. Drowned in the River Ouse.

(8) Died in York Military Hospital, March, 1917. Further particulars refused.

(9) Died at Wakefield, January 20th, 1918.

(10) Drowned, August 2nd, 1917. Had joined the Non-Combatant Corps after serving one term in prison.

(11) Left Wakefield without leave and died at home, November, 1917.

(12) Lingered till March, 1921. Finally died in hospital from the effects of imprisonment.

(13) An artist. Had disease of the heart, but declined medical examination on principle. Was discharged in six weeks. Died January 4th, 1917.

(14) Died at Red Roses Camp, Carmarthen, of influenza under terrible conditions of crowding and neglect. Peddieson strove to nurse the others in the epidemic till he collapsed himself.

ONE WHO DIED FOR PEACE.

The following account of the death of Paul Gillan in Winchester Prison was written shortly after I was released from that prison owing to my own breakdown in health. I was in the hospital ward with Gillan and watched him while he died :—

"Twelve men, all correct, sir."

The Governor of Winchester Prison acknowledged the salute of the officer in charge of the hospital, marched down the ward, and then on to the next place of call on his daily inspection.

It is essential to the régime of His Majesty's prisons that everything should be "all correct" at least twice daily when the Governor or Chief Warder makes a tour of the prison, visiting every department, and receiving from the officers in charge the number of prisoners under their supervision. These numbers are added together and compared with the grand total on the slate in the central hall, so that any attempt by a prisoner at escape or concealment would be detected at once.

When one has been on one's back in a prison hospital for a month, unable to read or sleep or eat, and forbidden to speak, one finds oneself taking an abnormal interest in the most trivial events : the Governor's inspection, the visit of the doctor, the arrival of a new patient — all such incidents become as exciting as the circus procession of our boyhood days.

On Tuesday, March 12th—I have cause to remember the date—as I lay longing for something to happen to revive my interest in life, which had somewhat flagged since the excitement engendered by the Governor's inspection, I was relieved to hear the rattle of keys at the hospital gate ; and on looking towards the door of the ward I saw that an officer was bringing in another C.O.

"One on, sir," he sang out to the warder in charge of the hospital, as he altered the number on the hospital slate from twelve to thirteen. Then it was that I saw Paul Leo Gillan for the first time. A frail, tottering figure ; jet-black hair which gave his wan face a ghastly whiteness ; eyes heavy and bloodshot. He staggered across the ward to a bed opposite my own, and as he struggled through the process of undressing, I could see that every movement of his body caused him pain. He was racked by a cough which seemed to become worse with every attack. His temperature was found to be 102 degrees, and he was treated for a feverish chill.

In the evening I was able to converse with him *via* a fellow-prisoner who was convalescent, and I discovered that he was an Irishman and a Roman Catholic. He based his objection to military service on his interpretation of the words of Jesus, and added that in any case he would not fight for the country that had treated Ireland worse than Germany had treated Belgium. Being a genuine case, he had, of course, been refused exemption by the Tribunal, and had spent some time in Wormwood Scrubs before being released to undertake work under the Home Office scheme at Wakefield. He was forty years of age when arrested ; and he was so weakened by his experience at Wormwood Scrubs that when he arrived at Wakefield Settlement he was allowed to lie in bed while sewing mailbags. After a few months of the Home Office work he came to the conclusion that the whole scheme of so-called "work of national importance" was merely a punitive measure, and he decided to refuse to continue the work. He was promptly recalled to the Army, court-martialled, and sent to Mutley Prison, where he adopted the work strike. While at Mutley he was given the maximum punishment for refusing to work ; and when, after ten months of restricted diet, solitary confinement, and complete disconnection with his friends outside, he was transferred to Winchester Prison, he was in a state bordering on collapse. The doctor treated him in his cell for some time, and then ordered his removal to the hospital.

That was his story as I got it from him during the absence of the warder in charge.

On the following day his temperature dropped below normal, and his cough became more dry and painful. The doctor and the hospital warder treated him with every possible kindness. But it was too late ; his treatment at Mutley had exhausted his reserve strength, leaving him helpless to struggle against an illness that a man of normal strength would probably overcome in a few weeks. On the Friday his state was painful in the extreme. All through the day and night he lay groaning and gasping for breath. From my bed I watched him sink lower and lower ; his face changed from white to an ashen grey. Pleurisy had now set in, and poultices were being applied at frequent intervals. He knew that he was very near the end. On the Saturday afternoon his groans and terrible struggles for breath became so distressing to the other inmates of the ward that the doctor ordered his removal to a cell in the corridor. The hospital orderly, a soldier prisoner, carried him tenderly out of the ward, and on the way he tried to cheer his burden.

"Cheer up, mate !" whispered the orderly. "When you get over this lot you'll get your discharge, certain."

"Yes," gasped poor Gillan, "I shall get my discharge—very soon now."

Everything was very still in the ward when he was carried out ; we were all listening to those short, rasping gasps coming from the cell outside. I found myself counting them ; then I lost count and tried to remember how long I had been in prison ; and I thought what a good thing would be it Iif could get my discharge in the same way—no more courts martial, no more "Escort and accused, 'shon !" no more prison. . . .

"Thirteen men, all correct, sir." The voice of the warder rose above the groans and gasps. The Chief was making his usual afternoon round. Everything was obviously "all correct" so far ; no prisoner had succeeded in escaping—yet. About 7.30 p.m. the doctor came again. By this time the gasps had become feeble, rapid sighs, and I listened to them with tense expectancy.

Yes, he was still breathing. One—two—three—four—five—six. . . . A sudden silence ; then a rattling of keys as the doctor hurried away. The hospital warder came into the ward and threw up his hands with an expressive gesture.

"Gone ! " he said, with something like awe in his voice. "Went off just like that" ; and he threw up his hands again. They carried the body into a spare room to await the inquest. As the door shut on all that remained of our comrade the officer in charge for the night came into the hospital on the first night round of inspection.

"Twelve men ; one dead 'un ; all correct, sir ! " said the hospital warder.

So Paul Gillan got his discharge.

CHAPTER VIII.

IN earlier chapters we have noted the Government's attempts to solve the problem of the War Resister by offering him various forms of alternative service. What the war mind could not understand was the position of those men who persisted in refusing to undertake such service and went to prison instead. As will be seen from the figures given in the previous chapter, only a minority of those who objected to war service took up what came to be known as the Absolutist position. It must be borne in mind, however, that it was no easy matter for young men to take that position. In the ranks of the No-Conscription Fellowship there was keen discussion of this question, and although the Fellowship endorsed the Absolutist position, it was clear that many sincere objectors to war service felt that they could not conscientiously refuse to undertake work organised by the civil authorities as an alternative to combatant service or other forms of military work.

The Absolutist took his stand on what is now generally regarded as the logical view that every form of alternative service offered by a Government in war-time is regarded by the Government as assisting in the prosecution of the war. Whatever kind of work was offered, it must of necessity mean releasing other men for war service. The logic of this position was tested by Clifford Allen, who, when asked if he would accept some form of alternative service, replied with an offer to continue his peace work. Needless to say the Tribunal refused his offer ! "Work of national importance" was the term applied by the Government to all forms of alternative service offered, and that fact was sufficient to justify the Absolutist's position. That position can best be illustrated by quoting from the statements made by representative War Resisters to the Tribunals. Here is an extract from A. Fenner Brockway's statement :—

"Suppose the State, in a time of grave economic distress, were to decide that every man and woman above sixty years of age was an unjustifiable burden upon the community and therefore ordered its young men to kill all persons who reached that age. It might be expected that many young men would conscientiously object to doing any such thing. ' Very well,' the State might say to them, ' We recognise your conscientious objection, but if you are to be excused from killing the old people you must at least consent to cremate their bodies, or perform some other duty which we consider to be of national importance.' To cremate the bodies would be of hygienic benefit to the whole community ; but might we not expect many young men to answer ' No ; the whole thing is diabolical, I will have nothing to do with it. If I consented to cremate the bodies, or to do any other work under such conditions, I should become a party to the crime by which they are put to death.' "

J. Scott Duckers, a prominent Liberal solicitor, who was equally strong in his opposition to all forms of alternative service—and even refused to appear before a Tribunal— summed up his position thus :—

"The only purpose which the Government could have in transferring me to another occupation would be that in their view I should then be most useful in helping to carry on the war. Being against the war, I want to stop it."

Stuart Beavis, one of the Absolutists sentenced to death in France and afterwards sent to Winchester Prison to serve a sentence of ten years' penal servitude, wrote as follows while on his way to prison :—

"I do not see how a man can logically accept ' work of national importance ' as a condition of his release. . . . As soon as one makes a condition of that sort it is tantamount to bargaining his right to dispose of his conscience, and it rather looks as though I shall have to stay in prison for the completion of my term. And even here I can see troubled waters ahead, as I cannot undertake to do work that is of a military nature, and then I shall make myself liable to all sorts of penalties and not be allowed the privilege of writing letters and receiving visits. . . . That will also make it highly improbable that I shall get any remission marks for good conduct, so I am making up my mind to go through some dark times. However, I am going to try to keep smiling, remembering that others have gone through worse for their fellows."

The unprejudiced person will say, "Well, surely that man was genuine, and was just the kind of man for whom the exemption was provided in the Conscription Act." That is the reasonable view. But, as somebody has said, in war-time "reason" is spelt with a "T." It was just this kind of War Resister who did *not* receive exemption. And while such men were refused exemption under the Conscience Clause, the

Tribunals were granting exemptions to beer-tasters, brewers' employees, printing operatives engaged by the Amalgamated Press in the production of *Comic Cuts* and other such journals, huntsmen, and many others on the ground that they were performing "work of national importance"!

In a letter to the Prime Minister, in August, 1916, setting out the position of the Absolutist, the National Committee of the No-Conscription Fellowship made the following statement :—

"These include many Quakers, and some of those who have already faced the death penalty in France, and are now undergoing periods of ten years' penal servitude. To them it is not the character or the conditions of the service offered that affects their decision. *It is not killing only to which they object : it is war and therefore militarism.* They believe it wrong to accept conditional exemption because they hold it to be a bargain with a *Military* Service Act, which to them is the most complete expression of militarism yet admitted in this country. They welcome the obligation of every man to serve the community, *but believe that their refusal to be a party to this Act is the highest form of service they can render.* It is these men of whom Mr. Lloyd George stated : ' I shall only consider the best means of making the path of that class a very hard one.' Thus, for the very reason that they cannot waive their conviction, they are to be subjected to prolonged persecution, expressly authorised by the Government with a view to breaking their determination to be loyal to their sense of right and wrong."

When Clifford Allen was handed over to the military

authorities, Bertrand Russell wrote a brilliant reply to Lloyd George, from which I quote the following :—

"There is a manly note of primitive ferocity about these words. They show the odd misconception of the nature of conscience which has been common to almost all our politicians. . . . Mr. Lloyd George seems to think that conscience can only *forbid* things : the kind that *enjoins* things is apparently unknown to him. Does he think that St. Paul would have been satisfied with a certificate excusing him from preaching paganism ? Does he think that Luther would have acquiesced in a dispensation from maintaining the doctrine of indulgences, on condition that he should preserve silence as to his objections to the doctrine ? Does he think that Joan of Arc would have accepted civil alternative service ? Would he himself have been willing to spend all his time during the Boer War growing cabbages ?

"All these parallels, and especially the last, are applicable to the case of Mr. Clifford Allen, and, in varying degrees, to the cases of the other men who will not accept alternative service. They believe that war is a crime and a disaster ; they cannot satisfy their consciences by a passive non-participation, but feel bound to do what they can to bring the nations to their point of view . . . A man who will not fight himself is bound in honour to avoid, if he can, any action which enables the Government to compel someone else to fight in his place. . . . The Government cannot break the movement which has been led by Mr. Clifford Allen, but they can advertise to the world his sincerity and courage, and their incapacity to understand the nature of a conscience which does not consist in isolated prohibitions but in a determination to serve mankind in every possible way . . ."

About this time a statement was issued by the Friends' Service Committee, entitled "The Absolutists' Objection to Conscription : An Appeal to the Conscience of the Nation."

"We appeal," said the statement, "not that these men should be released from prison, but rather that their fellow countrymen should understand the motives that prompt their action and should appreciate the unconquerable moral conviction that enables them to stand alone in the midst of a nation practically united in condemning them. We are not concerned so much for the sufferings of these men. Their letters abundantly prove that in the Army they have had opportunities for preaching the truth they hold, and these opportunities they value far beyond personal liberty. . . . If we are looking for any result from our appeal, it is that our fellow countrymen may recognise that these men honestly believe in a force stronger than physical force, in obedience to moral laws even when they conflict with the laws of the State, and in a whole world of spiritual values against which military conquests count for less than nothing.

"If the nations of Europe could really believe in these things, they would call a truce to all fighting and unite in a search for the better way. We hope for nothing less, in calling attention to the principles that inspire the absolute resistance to military service, than that the war, with its untold and untellable horrors, its degradations, should give way to the forces of reason, of negotiation, of mutual adjustments, of mutual forbearance—of love. *We are more anxious to stop the war—*

to get the men of Europe out of the trenches—than we are to get conscientious objectors out of prison . . .

" *There comes a time in the progress of society when the duty the citizen owes to his country is to disobey the commands of his Government. Such a time occurred in the early days of Quakerism, and the early Friends were faithful. We believe another time has come now when men must refuse military and national service in order to restore the ideal of international unity.*"

After giving particulars of the number of Absolutists then in prison and of their treatment, this dignified statement concluded :—

"We wish to state the case of these Absolutists as strongly and as clearly as possible, without desiring in the slightest degree to reflect on those who have felt it right to adopt another course. We feel that in this small company we have got to the very heart of the protest against militarism. . . . The Absolutist position offers the most effective challenge to the political and military aggression that threatens the nation. . . . The message of these men is a message of international brotherhood, a message that humanity is greater than any of its parts, and that allegiance to humanity is a higher duty than allegiance to a nation, a message that men should look beyond frontiers to the common Fatherhood of God, and the Brotherhood of Man. Could they withhold a message like this until the war is over ? In the faithful delivering of this message they are performing their highest national service. This is the claim of these Absolutist apostles of international peace."

The attitude of Mr. Lloyd George towards these men was so illogical that, looking back on it in these days of comparative sanity, one finds it difficult to understand how this erstwhile War Resister could have acted as he did. The problem for the Government of that day was a difficult one, it must be admitted. The Military Service Act contained the Conscience Clause which quite clearly allowed complete exemption to be granted to persons whose genuineness was established. The difficulty was, of course, how to tell a genuine conscientious objector from a mere "shirker." But Mr. Lloyd George's method was to make it easy for the "shirkers"—if there were any—to evade military service by accepting one or the other forms of alternative service. But the man who refused this way out—whose very refusal to accept such a way out was proof that his motive was not cowardice—was sent to prison. What Mr. Lloyd George said, in effect, was : "If you want to save your skin we will make the way easy. But if your object is, at whatever cost, to prove beyond a shadow of doubt that you are a genuine War Resister, we shall make your path a hard one."

But it was the Absolutist who kept the flag of Peace flying, and thus paved the way for the great world-wide War Resistance movement which stands to-day as a formidable and ever-growing bulwark against war.

MISFITS IN UNIFORM

WHAT'S HAPPENING OUTSIDE ?

A VISIT

CAN I STICK IT ?

PRISON SKETCHES BY AN IMPRISONED WAR RESISTER

CHAPTER IX.

REAPING THE HARVEST.

MR. LLOYD GEORGE maintained his vindictive attitude towards the Absolutists until April, 1919, five months after the Armistice, when those who had served two years or more were released. The last of the War Resisters were released in July of that year, their sentences having been commuted. In December, 1917, owing to the serious effect of imprisonment on the health of a number of the men, the Government agreed to release men whom the prison doctors regarded as unfit to endure further imprisonment, and from that date up to the general release, about 300 men broken in health were released by special order of the Home Secretary. In my own case my release was obtained by the prison doctor a few months before the Armistice, because an Absolutist in the next bed to me in the prison hospital (Paul Gillan) died, and he did not want to risk another death ; so I was sent home in the charge of a hospital warder, and my wife had to sign a receipt for my live body.

All through this struggle against militarism the hope that inspired the men in prison was that their witness would not be in vain, and that they might live to see their despised faith accepted by the very people who had acquiesced in their imprisonment. The imprisonment of War Resisters had resulted in world-wide publicity for their views, and it is no exaggeration to say that they did more effective peace propaganda as prisoners than they could have done as free men. The Government's persecution roused men like Lord Hugh Cecil, and many others who did not share the War Resisters' views, to great protests which were worth much to the country in that black period. (Even *The Times* was compelled, towards the end of 1917, to urge, in a leading article, that the punishment of these men should not be continued.)

A notable speech in defence of War Resisters was made by a soldier, Captain Gwynne, M.P., in the House of Commons on June 26th, 1917. Speaking against the motion to deprive War Resisters of their votes, he said :—

"These are people who are not a blight upon the community; they may very probably prove to be the very salt of the community. I am speaking now as one who has seen war. I think that everybody who has seen war has one governing desire, and that is to see war abolished from the world. *I am not at all sure that these people, whom we propose to reject as the outcasts of the State, may not be the best people to help in the fight to make an end of war.* There is one thing that nobody can deny them, and that is courage, the most difficult form of courage in the world, the courage of the individual against the crowd. That is a courage which every State will do well to protect and guard. That is the courage which, above all others, makes for freedom. It is for that that I desire to see these men electors, and that I vote for giving them votes— just exactly as I would give votes to the soldiers—because they are the people who have shown not merely physical courage, but because they have made civic responsibility their plea. They have shown a spirit of initiative. These people, in refusing to act, have taken action which must have been extremely difficult to take, and when we are told that the good of the nation is to be somehow impaired by allowing these men a voice in our national councils, I ask myself, What is ' the good of the nation ' ?   Are you going to advance the real interests of this country, or of any country, by stamping out such people from among your full citizens ?   Progress, as far as I can understand, comes not with the crowd, but with individuals.   Freedom in the last resort is won by individuals working against the crowd, and these are the people who make for freedom.   It is in the interests of freedom during a war that is fought, at all events professedly, for freedom that I resist this attempt to limit what is the exercise of their legal freedom, and what is, I think with the Noble Lord, the exercise of higher morals."

At the end of November, 1919, a great and memorable final Convention of the No-Conscription Fellowship was held at Devonshire House.   It was attended by 400 delegates from branches all over the country, and messages were received from groups of War Resisters in other countries.   Clifford Allen presided, and in a masterly address, summed up the lessons and experiences of the struggle.   At its conclusion, he moved the following dedicatory resolution, which was passed by the delegates standing in an impressive silence :—

"Throughout the war we have stood for the Brotherhood of Man, and in the name of that ideal have resisted conscription. We now reaffirm our unity of aim with those in all countries who have given their lives that they might serve the cause of freedom, but declare our belief that it is not by bloodshed that freedom can be won or militarism destroyed.

"We acclaim the new hope of human liberty now challenging ancient tyrannies in industry, within the State and between the nations, and dedicate the liberty we have regained to such service as shall contribute to the healing of the wounds inflicted by war, and to the building of a world rooted in freedom and enriched by labour that is shared by all.

"It is in this spirit that we go forth to meet new tasks, confident that through its long and bitter suffering mankind must yet come into the way of love."

* * *

Fourteen months later, on February 24th, 1921, the No More War Movement was founded at a conference held at the Penn Club, London, over which I presided, and which was attended by a number of people who had signed an Affirmation Against War, the originator of which was Miss T. W. Wilson, who had been one of the foremost women workers for peace during the war. The Provisional Committee set up was composed of Miss T. W. Wilson, Bertram Appleby, H. Runham Brown, A. Fenner Brockway, F. Fincham, and Wilfred Wellock. I was elected chairman, and Miss Beatrice C. M. Brown agreed to act as secretary. The conference appointed Wilfred Wellock to attend the Anti-Militarist Congress held at the Hague, during the following month. That was the first step towards getting into touch with War Resisters in other lands, and it was that step which led to the formation of the War Resisters' International.

The story of the growth of the War Resistance idea since that handful of people met at the Penn Club is an amazing one. During the war, news of what was happening in other belligerent countries was either distorted or suppressed, and the British War Resisters knew little or nothing of the War Resistance movement abroad. At times the British Press contained stories of German War Resisters being shot ; but these stories were cancelled out by others to the effect that in no other enemy country were there men who refused to take part in the war. But once the Press censorship was lifted at the end of the war, news began to trickle through from other countries which confirmed the view that in every country involved in the war, there were men who stood out against it. Actual numbers are impossible to estimate, as in no other country than Great Britain was the War Resistance movement organised effectively. But it is known that in Germany, Austria, Hungary, Russia, Bohemia, America, and even in France, there were men who refused to fight and suffered pretty much the same treatment as that meted out to British War Resisters. In Hungary, where there was a large number of Nazarenes who refused to serve in the army, there were wholesale shootings of these men. In Bohemia there was also considerable opposition to war service by the Young Czechs, and here, too, there was a relentless shooting of men who refused to fight.

In Germany there was a small body of men who opposed the war, and among them were Professor Foerster, of Munich, Professor Nicolai, of Berlin, Professor Sieper, Dr. Quidde and Professor Einstein. Professor Nicolai was imprisoned for his Pacifist utterances. The most exhaustive enquiries after the war failed to discover any case of a German War Resister being shot. Apart from a number of Nazarenes, "Adventists," and members of other religious sects with a definite anti-war basis, there were very few objectors. So far as can be ascertained, objectors to war service were offered non-combatant service, and one way of getting rid of those who refused to accept this alternative was to declare them insane and lock them up as lunatics.

In America, in spite of the assurance given by the Secretary for War, that in dealing with War Resisters brutalities such as had occurred in Great Britain would be avoided, those who resisted the American Conscription Act (and there were about 4,000) were in many cases treated abominably by the military authorities. War Resisters in the American Army were prodded with bayonets, chained to the doors of prison cells, immersed in filth, and in other ways maltreated. Most of the men eventually gave in to such treatment and accepted some form of non-combatant service. There was no organisation of the movement in America, and each man was left to struggle alone, or at least without the help of a body such as the No-Conscription Fellowship. Those who refused all form of service (their number was estimated at 500) were sentenced to long terms of imprisonment in military prisons, and in spite of President Wilson's "idealism" (both he and the War Secretary, Mr. Baker, were Liberals, and Mr. Baker, like Mr. Lloyd George, had once professed to be a Pacifist) it was not until the summer of 1920 that the last of the American Absolutists were released. John William Graham records the melancholy fact that in America, once the war madness had gripped the nation, not even the Churches raised a voice in protest against the treatment of these men until public opinion, in very shame, demanded their release. "And it would be the testimony of everyone concerned with the position of objectors," writes Mr. Graham, "that, with few exceptions, representatives of the Churches and the Y.M.C.A. were harder to deal with than the military themselves. Labour also in America was slower than in England to ask for amnesty, although on the whole Labour awakened before the Church."

In New Zealand between 300 and 400 men were imprisoned for refusing all war service. In Canada there were also men who resisted and were imprisoned, but we have no record of the number.

In Soviet Russia, under Lenin, the Absolutist position was recognised and provided for by the following decree :—

"Under exceptional cases, the Joint Council of Religious Groups and Communes may have resource to the All-Russian Central Executive Committee, with a view to securing complete freedom of service, without the substitution of other service, if it can be shown that such substitution is incompatible with religious convictions ; the proof to be taken from writings on the question and also from the personal life of the individual concerned."

It will be noticed that this decree applied only to persons holding definite religious views, and would not meet the case of the objector who was not a member of a religious body. But it must be said that Lenin was more sympathetic than Lloyd George in his attitude towards those who objected to serve in the Red Army. In response to representations made to him by various religious bodies, he allowed the Council of

Religious Groups to act as the Tribunal for testing the genuineness of conscientious objection. Before the Revolution there were about a thousand objectors in prison. These men were set free by the Revolution, but the whole question was raised again when the Red Army was being recruited. In some parts of Russia removed from the Central Government, it is alleged that about fifteen War Resisters were shot after the Revolution ; and, unfortunately, there are still many men in the prisons of Soviet Russia who have refused service in the Red Army. In Russia to-day exemption from military service is given only to those who can prove that before the revolution they were members of a religious body including a conscientious objection to war in its articles of belief.

* * *

Much valuable information was gathered by Wilfred Wellock during his visit to the Anti-Militarist Congress at the Hague, and when he came back and gave his report, the No More War Movement took steps to get in touch with anti-militarist groups in other lands. H. Runham Brown, with the whole-hearted assistance of Martha Steinitz, of Berlin, undertook this important work, with the result that the War Resisters International was formed. This body held its second triennial conference at Sontagsberg (Austria) in August of this year (1928), when affiliated organisations from twenty-one countries were represented. A. Fenner Brockway (chairman) presided, and fraternal delegates were sent by the International Co-operative Movement, the Women's International League, the Ex-Servicemen's International, and other bodies. The Socialist Mayor of Vienna gave an official welcome to the delegates. The following summary of the chairman's address, which appeared in the *Daily Herald*, shows how the idea of War Resistance has spread throughout the world :—

"Mr. Fenner Brockway (chairman) said that no idea was making greater progress than that of War Resistance. In Britain the Labour Party, the General Council of the Trades Union Congress, the Co-operative Congress, and the I.L.P. were all committed to it. In Germany, which had been regarded as the home of militarist ideas, there was now a mass movement towards War Resistance.

"In practically every conscript country in Europe, young men were in prison for refusing war service, and many Governments were introducing schemes of alternative service for conscientious objectors.

"War Resisters were not, however, concerned about securing exemption for themselves. They wanted to end war for everyone. They believed that the most effective means of ridding the world of war was to create a war-resisting psychology among the peoples.

"That psychology, as it became strong, would lead Governments to pursue peace policies, would find expression in the construction of peace machinery for arbitration, would undermine the force upon which capitalist imperialism was based, and would overthrow any Government which dared to resort to war. It would mean the final triumph of mankind over war."

*   *   *

This world-wide growth of the War Resistance movement can truly be said to have had its origin in the stand made by the British War Resisters. When the news of that stand got to other countries, it encouraged the peace forces everywhere to unite on the common basis of a personal refusal to take any part in a future war. The first response came from disillusioned Germany, where a great cry went up from the people, "*Nie Wieder Krieg* ! " ("No More War ! "). If my memory is not at fault, this slogan was adopted in Great Britain and Germany almost simultaneously ; and at the Penn Club conference where the British Section of the No More War Movement was born, those present were confirmed in their resolve to adopt the slogan as the title of the movement by the exhibition of German posters bearing the slogan, which had been sent to Miss Wilson by friends in Germany. The German No More War Movement was founded by Dr. Robert Pohl and G. W. Myer, two Germans who were interned in Great Britain during the war, and took the news of the British Movement back to Germany. America then took up the cry, and soon after the publication of *No More War*, the monthly organ of the movement, an American journal was published with the same title to voice the views of a similar movement in that country.

The Declaration signed by every member of the No More War Movement is as follows :—

> *War is a crime against humanity. I am therefore determined—*
>
> (1) *Not to take part in any war, international or civil ;*
> (2) *To work for Total Disarmament, the removal of all causes of war, and the establishment of a New Social and International Order based on the Pacifist principle of Co-operation for the Common Good.*

Very soon after the formation of the Movement, it became obvious that its rapid growth demanded effective organisation and adequate office facilities to cope with the work of building up the movement and making its voice heard in the country. In 1925 Lucy A. Cox became General Secretary, and Fenner Brockway, Chairman, a position he held until the annual conference of 1928, when he felt that he ought to make way for "new blood," and Harold Morland was unanimously elected to the office. Towards the end of 1926, the Movement was further strengthened by the appointment of Walter H. Ayles as Organising Secretary. From a few hundreds, the Movement has grown into thousands, with branches all over the country. It is the spear-head of the *real* Peace movement in this country. Its propaganda has resulted in the adoption of the War Resistance idea by the organised Workers' Movement. It has raised the issue among the Churches, with the result that there is now a strong and ever-growing body of Christian ministers who take their stand against all war. In August, 1928, an International Union of Anti-Militarist Clergymen was formed at Amsterdam, pledged to use all its influence against war. Dr. Hector Macpherson, a member of the National Committee of the No More War Movement, is chairman of the Executive of that body.

The activities of the No More War Movement have also resulted in Total Disarmament motions being moved in the British House of Commons on several occasions, and to-day there are 116 members of the House who have voted for that policy. The policy of personal resistance to war is now openly advocated by leaders of public opinion in journals which, during the war, were reviling War Resisters. In the early part of 1928, Mr. H. G. Wells was allowed to say this in the *Sunday Express* :—

"The most effective resistance to the approach of another great war lies in the expressed determination of as many people as possible that they will have nothing to do with it, that they will not fight in it, work for it, nor pay taxes when it comes, whatever sort of war it may be."

In his recent book, *The Open Conspiracy*, Mr. Wells declares :—

"From the outset the Open Conspiracy will set its force against Militarism. There is a plain present need for the organisation now, before war comes again, of an open and explicit refusal to serve in any war . . . The time for a conscientious objection to war service is manifestly now, and not after the onset of war. People who have acquiesced in a belligerent foreign policy by silence right up to the onset of war have little to complain of if they are then compelled to serve. And a refusal to participate with one's country in warfare is a preposterously incomplete gesture unless it is rounded off by the deliberate advocacy of a world *pax*, a world economic control . . ."

If Mr. Wells had been asked to sum up the aim and object of the No More War Movement, he could not have done it better. One of the most effective pieces of *real* peace work undertaken during the past year has been Mr. Arthur Ponsonby's "Peace Letter" campaign, in which the No More War Movement has co-operated whole-heartedly. In spite of limited resources, and a boycott by most of the Press in the country, Mr. Ponsonby has secured about 130,000 signatures to the following "Peace Letter" to the Prime Minister :—

"Sir,—We, the undersigned, convinced that all disputes between nations are capable of settlement either by diplomatic negotiation or by some form of International Arbitration, hereby solemnly declare that we shall refuse to support or render war service to any Government which resorts to arms."

The "Peace Letter" idea has been adopted in Germany, and in the limited area of Saxony over 200,000 signatures have been secured. Both in this country and in Germany huge public meetings have been addressed in connection with this campaign.

Among other striking declarations in favour of personal resistance to war was the following, made by Mr. H. M. Tomlinson, the well-known war correspondent, in the course of an article in *Harper's Magazine* at the end of last year :—

"Whoever may be the enemy, whatever may be the reason for a war, good citizens can have no part in it. I for one will not serve, will not help, will not pay, and am prepared to take the consequences."

Mr. H. W. Nevinson, another famous war correspondent, was equally emphatic in an article written about the same time, in which he said :—

"All who take the oath of resistance must expect the treatment of other martyrs, but for myself I see no other way to peace, but this concentration in the form of a general strike against the war-mongers."

Yet another war correspondent, Sir Philip Gibbs, as early as 1915, in his book, *The Soul of the War*, in which he gave as much of his impressions of the war at first-hand as he was allowed to give in war-time, wrote this message to the people of the world :—

"There will be no hope of peace until the peoples of the world recognise their brotherhood and refuse to be led to the shambles for mutual massacre. If there is no hope of that, if, as some students of life hold, war will always happen because life is a continual warfare, and one man only lives at the expense of another, then there is no hope, and all the ideals of men striving for the progress of mankind, all the dreams of poets and the sacrifices of scientists are utterly vain and foolish, and pious men should pray God to touch this planet with a star and end the folly of it all."

In another equally striking passage in the same book, Sir Philip Gibbs wrote :—

"More passionate than any other emotion that has stirred me through life, is my conviction that any man who has seen these things must, if he has any gift of expression, and any human pity, dedicate his brain and heart to the sacred deity of preventing another war like this. A man with a pen in his hand, however feeble it may be, must use it to tell the truth about the monstrous horror, to etch its images of cruelty into the brains of his readers, and to tear down the veils by which the leaders of the people try to conceal its obscenities. The conscience of Europe must not be lulled to sleep again by the old phrases about ' the ennobling influence of war ' and its ' purging fires.' It must be shocked by the stark reality of this crime in which all humanity is involved, so that from all the peoples of the civilised world there will be a great cry of rage and horror if the spirit of militarism raises its head again and demands new sacrifices of blood and life's beauty."

That was the message which the War Resisters were preaching to the people from prison cell and guard-room during the Great War. Then they were only a mere handful. To-day they are numbered in their thousands throughout the world. Within a few months of their release from prison their message had been heard by a sufficient number of their fellow countrymen to bring about a nation-wide revolt against a threatened war between Great Britain and Soviet Russia.

As the last page of this book is being written, the Kellogg Pact is being signed by the representatives of fifteen nations. Despite its "reservations" and evasions of the vital question of disarmament, the Pact is a gesture which, if the peoples of the world are wise, they can translate into something more tangible. But the only real safeguard against war lies in a people pledged to resist all war ; and those who stood firm in their resistance to war during those dark days of 1914-1918 prepared the way for the Peace forces of to-day.

Why I Believe in The No More War Movement

By Leaders of Thought and Action in all Circles

PROF. FREDERICK SODDY, M.A., D.Sc.
(*The Well-known Scientist*).

The reason why I support any movement working towards the abolition of war is because I believe that the next great war will destroy the white civilisation.

(Signed) FREDERICK SODDY.

S. MARGERY FRY, M.A.
(*Principal of Somerville College, Oxford*).

Because I believe that war is a greater curse than any evil men hope to prevent by fighting. Civilisation must end war, or war will end civilisation.

(Signed) S. MARGERY FRY.

HENRY T. GILLETT, M.D.

Because war either destroys the enemies' minds or hardens them into hate. War settles nothing ; it is futile and wasteful.

Truth, friendship and liberty are best served by hostile parties putting all their cards on the table and patiently discussing differences in an endeavour to understand one another.

(Signed) HENRY T. GILLETT, M.D. (Lond.).

ROGER SOLTAU, M.A.

(Joint General Secretary, International Fellowship of Reconciliation).

Because war has been proved to be futile as a method of settling political disputes, and disastrous in its moral and economic consequences ; because it fails to remove the fears, hatreds and greeds from which it springs, and, lastly, because it is in flagrant contradiction with the Christian ethic, and with God's method of dealing with evil, which method is revealed in the Cross of Christ.

(Signed) ROGER H. SOLTAU, M.A.

PROF. HAROLD J. LASKI, M.A.

(Professor Political Science, University of London).

The weapons now at the disposal of conflict make war and civilisation incompatible. Moreover, the reorganisation entailed in its onset makes it not merely opposed to the democratic organisation of society, but also certain to breed habits of violence in the population incompatible with social good.

Its cost, further, is now so great that the reforms, economic, social and political, essential to the good life cannot be attained except in terms of peace.

(Signed) HAROLD J. LASKI.

DR. ERNEST B. LUDLAM
(of Edinburgh University, M.A., Cambridge ; D.Sc., Liverpool; F.R.S.E.).

From the personal view, because I believe that the application of the teaching of Jesus is the chief purpose in life of all who presume to call themselves Christians ; it is merely conventional morality which sanctions war.

From the wider aspect, because I believe the time has now come for educated democracy to denounce war, and all preparation for it, as a ghastly crime against humanity.

(Signed) ERNEST BOWMAN LUDLAM.

A. BARRATT BROWN, M.A.
(Principal of Ruskin College, Oxford).

To disarm one's self is the best way to disarm opposition. It is because the No More War Movement stands for personal disarmament as the most effective means of abolishing war that I give it my warmest support.

(Signed) A. BARRATT BROWN.

MARGARET MACMILLAN
(The Well-known Educationist).

I believe in the No More War Movement because it shifts the real battle of life to the real battle-ground.

War means reversion *always*. Suffering may purify, but mutual destruction spells relapse. To fight the spiritual battle against evil in Self is our real task to-day on this planet.

(Signed) MARGARET MACMILLAN.

THE LATE ARTHUR BOURCHIER, M.A.
(*Actor and Author*).

The prime and greatest essential for the abolition of war is the supersession of Imperialistic capitalism by a system of Socialist communities organised internationally on a world basis.

And it is because I am convinced that the No More War Movement recognises this fact, and that such is always its implied objective, that I believe in it.

Every wish for continued success !

(Signed) ARTHUR BOURCHIER.

DR. A. D. LINDSAY, M.A.
(*Master of Balliol, Oxford*).

I could sign your declaration if the first clause ("not to support or take part in any war, international or civil") were omitted. I am not clear that there might not be an occasion in which I should not have to feel that taking part in war was the lesser of two evils.

Although I am therefore precluded from signing your declaration, I do at the same time recognise that as a matter of history great and signal evils like war have usually been stopped by people who took an absolute and often unreasoning stand against them, and said : "We don't care about the various considerations which may be urged in the opposite direction ; this thing is so evil that we will have no part or lot in it."

(Signed) A. D. LINDSAY.

C. T. CRAMP

(Industrial Secretary, N.U.R.).

Because war is absolutely unnecessary ; because the people who have to fight in the wars have absolutely no control over their conduct ; because war is barbaric ; because war is expensive and the bulk of the expense both in life and money is always paid in the end by the workers.

The last war truly illustrates the Biblical quotation : "Unto him that hath shall be given, and from him that hath not shall be taken even that which he hath." Let those who want war fight. Impose this condition and there will not be any more war.

(Signed) C. T. CRAMP.

DR. HUGH DALTON, M.A., M.P.

(Reader in Economics in the University of London ; Member National Executive of the Labour Party).

Because the middle-aged and elderly people who make wars don't fight themselves (that might make an amusing spectacle), but only drive innocent young life, which is the most precious thing in the world, to terror and agony and death ; because there is no cause of dispute between the peoples of the world which cannot be settled by peaceful means, and because a programme of constructive internationalism, including all-round disarmament, arbitration and economic co-operation is practical politics as soon as the electors choose to make it so.

(Signed) HUGH DALTON.

BEN TURNER

(The Well-known Textile Trade Union Lrader).

I believe most thoroughly in the "No More War Movement."

It must not be alone lip service. There should be no "ifs" and "buts" about it.

There is no morality in war, and a nation should uphold morality.

(Signed) BEN TURNER.

MARGARET LLEWELYN DAVIES

(Ex-General Secretary, Women's Co-operative Guild; Ex-President, Co-operative Congress).

Because personal refusal of war service by the *people* will goad governments into arbitration, disarmament and loyalty to the League of Nations. Also, because it is impossible without *total* war resistance to cut at the roots of military propaganda and the perversion of science, and to achieve the general outlook which regards war, like slavery, as an outworn barbarity. Nor, otherwise, can men's energies be directed to the all-absorbing constructive efforts which Peace demands.

(Signed) MARGARET LLEWELYN DAVIES.

MURIEL COUNTESS DE LA WARR.

To me war seems the negation of Christianity and Brotherhood. As individuals, we have so far advanced that in disputes with one another we discuss the matter reasonably and, if necessary, leave the final decision to a third party, whether in the Law Courts or otherwise.

Surely it is an anomaly that in international affairs we still accept the doctrine that might is right ; yet it is that doctrine which inspires our naval and military programmes.

We want a band of men and women who realise and are prepared to teach that, at the stage we have reached, there is no glory in war, and, further, that no disputes are ever really settled by it.

(Signed) M. DE LA WARR.

THE MARQUIS OF TAVISTOCK.
(*Chairman, Copec Committee*).

Because the time has come when war, as a means of settling a dispute between civilised countries, will always be a greater danger and a greater evil than any alternative course.

If steps are taken to put and keep the peoples of the different nations in direct touch with one another, so that their passions can no longer be stirred by false propaganda playing on ignorance, there will be no danger of one country doing serious injustice to its neighbour.

(Signed) TAVISTOCK.

JOHN HILL
(General Secretary, Boiler-makers' Society).

Wars are hatched in secret by a few in high places, to satisfy the lust for power or to further enrich the wealthy. The common people pay the price by the sacrifice of their lives and the degradation of their dependants, and only long after do the common people learn the truth, if they ever learn it. Wars are forced on the peoples by wholesale fraud and misrepresentation. The people do not make war. They should therefore refuse to fight or provide supplies, and demand that all international differences be referred to an international tribunal.

(Signed) JOHN HILL.

RHYS J. DAVIES, M.P.
(Ex-Under Secretary for Home Affairs).

I think it was the poet Shelley who said, in his "Queen Mab," that "War is a statesman's game and the priest's delight." The poet was not quite correct, because statesmen can neither make wars nor priests pray for their success without the support of the people.

I have come to the conclusion, therefore, very definitely, that no Government can either declare a war or wage one unless public opinion is favourable. It is imperative, therefore, that all those who oppose wars should support any *organised* movement for peace ; hence my reason for backing with all my heart the "No More War Movement" in this country.

(Signed) RHYS J. DAVIES.

MRS. BARBARA AYRTON GOULD.

I believe that the only way to prevent war is to have an educated body of public opinion which is so large, and so definitely opposed to all war, that it is able to check the great surge of hysterical feeling which sweeps over the people, when a calculating Government backed by a Jingo press, calls upon the patriotism of the nation to save the country by a bloody war. This body of public opinion can only be created by the steady work of the No More War Movement.

(Signed) BARBARA AYRTON GOULD.

HAMILTON FYFE

(*Late Editor, "Daily Herald," and War Correspondent on five fronts*, 1914-1918).

Because I have seen war.

(Signed) HAMILTON FYFE.

E. ROFFE THOMPSON, M.A.

(*Editor, "John Bull"*).

I believe in the "No More War" Movement because I believe in the future of civilisation, and another war would hurl an already tottering civilisation into utter and barbaric ruin.

War is the negation of reason, and the last resort of the ineffective statesman and the blundering bully. There never was a good war any more than there was ever a just war. War will kill us unless we kill war, and we shall never kill war until we say flatly and finally, "We will not fight."

(Signed) E. R. THOMPSON.

139

EVELYN SHARP
(Authoress and Journalist).

Because it implies an active and not a negative pacifism. The definite pledge that binds its members is not one to be lightly made or lightly broken ; and the existence of such a body of men and women is an educational power between wars, and serves as a perpetual discouragement of the forces that lead to war.

(Signed) EVELYN SHARP.

EMILY PHIPPS, B.A.
(Barrister-at-Law ; Editor of the "Victorian Teacher" ; Past President of the National Union of Women Teachers).

One of my reasons is the hideous cruelty war inflicts on animals, particularly horses. Whatever the dispute which is the pretext for war, it is not the animals, dispute ; they are entirely in our power, and we have no right to cause them suffering in the settlement of our quarrels.

(Signed) EMILY PHIPPS.

MRS. H. M. SWANWICK, M.A.

War has become an anachronism. When we concentrate all our efforts on co-operation we shall cease to think and talk about war or to prepare for it. There is no conceivable dispute which would not be better solved by arbitration than by war.

(Signed) H. M. SWANWICK.

WHY I BELIEVE IN THE NO MORE WAR MOVEMENT

JAMES HASLAM

*(Principal of C.W.S. Press Agency and Publicity Department ;
Editor "People's Year Book," "The Journalist," etc.).*

I believe in this Movement because, if it were successful
it would remove one of the most brutal obstructions to
continuous social progress. The greatest price we pay for war
is not in more taxation, or even in the loss of life on the fields
of battle, but in the demoralisation of the race.

(Signed) JAMES HASLAM.

ASHLEY DUKES

(Author and Playwright).

If there is one thing stupider than war itself, it is the
military mind. The nation that goes to war, as we know to
our cost, surrenders its intelligence "for the duration." It
hands over not only the practical management of affairs, but
also its entire social life, to a number of persons in red tabs
whose ideas are obsolete, whose vision is obscure and whose
administrative power is negligible.

These military persons cannot even win battles, much less
wars ; and in the end the politicians have to win their wars for
them, because the career of politics is conditional upon a
certain measure of success. In brief, the politicians cannot
afford to lose wars, but the military commanders can—and do.
Their ambition is to carry on the struggle until everybody
loses, and then after a brief interval start again. Let us resist
them, in the name of our common wits.

(Signed) ASHLEY DUKES.

141

CANON F. LEWIS DONALDSON, M.A.
(*Canon of Westminster*).

Because the No More War Movement stands for Permanent Peace.

Because it proclaims that the "next war" is being made or *prevented* NOW, that it is useless to agitate for peace when war is imminent. The agitation must be long beforehand.

Because Peace does not "happen." Like war Peace must be *made*. "Blessed are the peace-makers." Peace must be worked for; it requires watchfulness, political knowledge and education. The price of Peace, like that of liberty, is eternal vigilance. The N.M.W.M. is an active agency, ceaselessly working for the conversion of the people in the cause of Peace.

Because the N.M.W.M. commits us to a definite personal act of faith in the possibility of the abolition of war, and counters in the nations the triple enemies of peace, ignorance, fear and competition, by knowledge, faith and co-operation.

(Signed) F. LEWIS DONALDSON.

LAURENCE HOUSMAN
(*Author and Playwright*).

Because evolution shows that the species which cannot adapt itself to changing conditions goes under. War helped primitive man to develop; but steadily, with the growth of civilisation, its drawbacks outweighed its advantages, and have now become embracingly destructive. Civilisation cannot survive the further development of war. To-day only sentimentalists approve of it; and I dislike sentimental suicide.

(Signed) LAURENCE HOUSMAN.

THE HON. LADY BARLOW

Because it is being worked by young people here and abroad.

Because it is based on the command, "Thou shalt not kill."

Because many in the Movement have suffered for their faith in Peace. (Signed) ANNA BARLOW.

CANON CHARLES E. RAVEN, D.D.

(Canon of Liverpool and Chaplain to the King).

For two main reasons, one personal, the other general. Personally because I took part in the World War believing that it was to end war. Many of my friends gave their lives for that ideal. We were perhaps mistaken in our means ; our end remains, and is for me an obligation to the dead.

Generally, because war is a manifestation of evil against which all people of good-will could and should combine. Christianity, commonsense, and recent experience testify that it is the wrong method of settling disputes.

(Signed) CHARLES E. RAVEN.

REV. LEYTON RICHARDS, M.A.

(Minister, Carr's Lane Church, Birmingham).

Because it acts on the principle that the only way to realise an ideal in the world at large is to embody it in our own life and bear the consequences of our fidelity.

The "fools" of one generation are usually found to be the wise men of the next, and they only can save the world from future war, who in the present will dare to be "fools" for the sake of the Prince of Peace.

(Signed) LEYTON RICHARDS.

143

LADY PARMOOR

I am convinced that all war is contrary to the spirit and teaching of Christ.

The enormous development of the power of armaments both during and since the Great War has brought mankind within measurable distance of destruction.

The League of Nations now provides procedure for the peaceful settlement of international disputes.

(Signed) MARIAN E. PARMOOR.

REV. HUMPHREY CHALMERS, M.A.
(*Baptist Minister, Warrington, Lancs.*).

I believe in the No More War Movement because war is morally wrong, and a denial of Christianity. Victory, however high the initial ideals of a war may be, goes to those achieving most murders, and inflicting the most unbearable cruelties. War can only cease when the people refuse to be the tools by whom this devilry becomes profitable to the war-makers.

(Signed) HUMPHREY CHALMERS.

MAUDE ROYDEN
(*Minister of the Guild House, London*).

It is difficult for anyone who has lived through 1914-1918 to understand how anyone can help believing in "No More War Movement" ; but it is urgent that *all who believe should act*, for already a new generation arises to whom that horror is no more than a faint memory.

(Signed) A. MAUDE ROYDEN.

REV. JOHN E. McINTYRE, M.A.

The only values which war is supposed to defend, war itself destroys—life, goods, honour, truth, goodness, love.

The only way to end war is to stop fighting and preparations for fighting. "Come out of that," you who love your fellows.

(Signed) JOHN E. McINTYRE.

PROF. CECIL JOHN CADOUX, M.A., D.D.

(of Yorkshire Independent College ; author of "The Early Christian Attitude to War.").

I believe in it because war is the worst of the many dangers that threaten mankind to-day, because it can be stopped effectively only by the refusal of convinced men to take part in it, and because such refusal is a quite clear (though negative) implicate of that whole way of life commended to us and enjoined upon us by God through Jesus Christ.

(Signed) CECIL JOHN CADOUX.

REV. T. RHONDDA WILLIAMS, M.A.

(of Brighton).

Because war must be stopped if civilisation is to survive, and because governments can, and always do abstain from war when they know the people are not prepared to fight. Let them know that we are never going to be prepared, and they will find other means of settling disputes.

(Signed) T. RHONDDA WILLIAMS.

145

MRS. C. R. BUXTON.

It is astounding that so many people who experienced the hell of the last war seem content to drift into another. The mass of people smoke their pipes and do nothing to save their children from what will be a far worse hell even than the last. Read "When London Burns" by Sydney Potter (supplied by I.L.P.). (Signed) DOROTHY F. BUXTON.

MRS. BARTON, J.P.
(*General Secretary, Women's Co-operative Guild*).

Because I believe it wrong to take the life of another.

Because I believe all disputes should be settled by reason, which gives the weakest the right to their point of view, and not by brute force, which is tyranny, and gives no real settlement.

Because we need the inventive and scientific mind, which is rare, turned towards developments for the happiness and welfare of humanity.

(Signed) ELEANOR BARTON, J.P.

REV. HENRY C. CARTER, M.A.
(*Congregational Minister, Cambridge*).

War will cease when enough people see that it is so wrong that nothing can ever justify it, and decide to act on this conviction whatever governments or public opinion may say. When men cease doing wrong, their way is cleared for seeing and doing right. The solution of problems which war now offers to solve will not be found until men abjure war. That is why I believe in the No More War Movement.

(Signed) H. C. CARTER.

REV. A. HERBERT GRAY, D.D.
(*Student Christian Movement*).

I believe in the No More War Movement because as I see things, unless it is successful, there will be no more civilisation. All our efforts in other directions to achieve a finer civilisation depend upon the securing for the world a foundation of peace. It is to my mind clearly the first necessity for all mankind.

(Signed) A. HERBERT GRAY.

REV. W. H. HAMILTON, M.A.
(*Minister of Middle United Free Church, Greenock ; Chief of the Greatheart Order of World-Friendship*).

It is a strong stand for ideal things, and it faces a hard task valiantly. Recognising that its thesis is arguable—as every progressive proposition is—and difficult to establish practically, I must still side with its exponents and advocates against all that (within me or around) urges the easier and shorter and (in the long run) fatal view. My own hope is in the children of all nations learning to know, and to know about, each other ; and in the encouraging growth of my Greatheart Order of World-Friendship (121, George Street, Edinburgh) and allied movements in many countries. The central aim of the No More War Movement has fellow-crusaders full of hope, although following a variety of methods and commanded by varying pledges.

(Signed) W. H. HAMILTON.

PROF. LASCELLES ABERCROMBIE, D.Litt.
(*Leeds University*).

We now know how to make war. By no possible consideration can war now be turned from its logical development: not hostile armies and navies, but hostile *nations* will be its objective. The real enemy forces henceforward will be the civilian populations : that is now well understood, and we understand also how to deal with hostile civilian populations. Destroy their towns, make transport impossible, contaminate water supply, and so on. War in the air has not only made all this possible, but necessary ; because whichever side does not do it first, invites its enemy to do it. No government dare resist the temptations of science. Both sides will start by disclaiming any intention of attacking the civilians, well knowing that the one that does so most effectively will win the war ; and the side that does it first will do it most effectively. Both sides will be ruined ; the slaughter will be quite purposeless ; and civilisation will finish so far as we are concerned.

(Signed) LASCELLES ABERCROMBIE.

REV. WILLIAM MORISON, D.D.
(*of Edinburgh*).

One morning during the war I was walking with my grandchildren through Princes Street Gardens, when we came on a body of recruits at bayonet practice. Pointing to the crowd of churches with their spires that surrounded us, I said, *"Either they must abolish this, or this will abolish them."* The churches can do it if they have a mind.

(Signed) WILLIAM MORISON.

ARNOLD S. ROWNTREE.

I welcome every effort to outlaw war. Let us realise, however, that we must be positive, as well as negative. "The test of friendship is proximity," and it is a few of us who can stand that searching test. But we must try.

(Signed) ARNOLD S. ROWNTREE.

REV. A. W. WARDLE
(*Wesleyan Minister, Blackburn*).

I support the N.M.W.M. because I believe that war is utterly and irremediably bad—the negation of everything that Christ stands for, and must therefore be unflinchingly and uncompromisingly resisted and opposed. Christ was manifested that He might destroy the works of the Devil.

(Signed) A. W. WARDLE.

MISS EFFIE RYLE, M.A.
(*National Adult School Union and Women's Warden, Avoncroft College, Offenham*).

I believe in the No More War Movement because (1) all to whom Christ's message has appealed are bound to live and work for the peace of the world.

(2) This means personal refusal to share in war—or preparation for war ; active work for disarmament, as the only real safeguard against war.

(3) A personal promise makes people *think*—and it has been lack of thought, as much as wrong thought, that has hitherto let us drift into wars.

(Signed) EFFIE RYLE, M.A.

No Truce to the Fight for Peace!

The pioneer of pacifism who suffered persecution during the Great War and the ex-soldier who has determined "Never Again ! " are to-day banded together by their common creed of war resistance in the

NO MORE WAR MOVEMENT

Thousands of others are joining them—women who are striving to save their homes and families from the havoc of war while there is yet time, Christians who see that faithful following of Christ lies along the path of peace, young people determined that their generation shall be saved from destruction, politicians who realise that plans for the world's welfare can never come to fruition without peace.

BUT WHAT OF YOURSELF ?

Are you a member of that noble fellowship that sets the ploughshare before the sword, the child before the warrior, the home before the citadel, brotherhood before conflict ? Can you honour the pledge of the No More War Movement ?

"War is a crime against humanity ; I am therefore determined :—

1. not to support or take part in any war, international or civil ;

2. to work for total disarmament, the removal of all causes of war, and the establishment of a new social and international order based upon the pacifist principle of co-operation for the common good."

Send your pledge now to the GENERAL SECRETARY, NO MORE WAR MOVEMENT, 11, DOUGHTY STREET, LONDON,W.C.1

MEN AND WOMEN WHO HAVE
SUFFERED FOR

PEACE

SHOULD GET THEIR PEACE
NEWS THROUGH

"NO MORE WAR"

THE ONLY PAPER IN ENGLAND
PLEDGED TO

PEACE

*It is published by the No More War
Movement, at 11, Doughty Street, London,
W.C.1, and costs one penny per copy or one
shilling and sixpence post free for twelve
months.*

THE
BLACKFRIARS
PRESS LTD.
Smith-Dorrien Road
L E I C E S T E R

DATE DUE

DEMCO 38-297